CW01307971

PICKLEBALL BASICS

FUNDAMENTAL TECHNIQUES AND RULES FOR CONFIDENCE, FITNESS AND SOCIAL PLAY

LATRICIA MAY

Copyright © 2024 Latricia May. All rights reserved.

The content within this book may not be reproduced, duplicated, or transmitted without direct written permission from the author or the publisher.

Under no circumstances will any blame or legal responsibility be held against the publisher, or author, for any damages, reparation, or monetary loss due to the information contained within this book, either directly or indirectly.

Legal Notice:

This book is copyright protected. It is only for personal use. You cannot amend, distribute, sell, use, quote, or paraphrase any part of the content within this book, without the consent of the author or publisher.

Disclaimer Notice:

Please note the information contained within this document is for educational and entertainment purposes only. All effort has been expended to present accurate, up-to-date, reliable, and complete information. No warranties of any kind are declared or implied. Readers acknowledge that the author is not engaged in the rendering of legal, financial, medical, or professional advice. The content within this book has been derived from various sources. Please consult a licensed professional before attempting any techniques outlined in this book.

By reading this document, the reader agrees that under no circumstances is the author responsible for any losses, direct or indirect, that are incurred as a result of the use of the information contained within this document, including, but not limited to, errors, omissions, or inaccuracies.

TABLE OF CONTENTS

Introduction   7

1. THE ORIGINS AND ESSENTIALS OF PICKLEBALL   11
   Tracing the Lines: The Birth and Spread of Pickleball   12
   Choosing Your Gear: A Comprehensive Guide to Pickleball Equipment   15
   Understanding Pickleball Courts: Layout and Specifications   19
   The Rules of the Game: An Easy Guide for Beginners   22
   Essential Pickleball Terminology: Slang and Lingo Decoded   25
   Setting up Your First Game: A Step-by-Step Guide   28

2. PREPARING TO PLAY: PHYSICAL AND MENTAL READINESS   31
   Warm-Ups and Cool-Downs: Essential Exercises for Pickleball   32
   Physical Ability: Building Endurance, Strength, Flexibility, and Agility for Better Play   37
   The Mental Game: Psychological Tips for Pickleball Success   43
   Injury Prevention and Management in Pickleball   47

3. MASTERING BASIC TECHNIQUES   53
   The Art of the Serve: Techniques and Tips   53
   Mastering the Return: Strategies to Start Strong   58
   The Volley: Timing and Technique   60
   Perfecting the Pickleball Dink: Why and How   62

Developing a Powerful Backhand 65
Footwork Fundamentals: Moving Efficiently
on the Court 68

4. ADVANCED SKILLS AND STRATEGIES 71
   Strategic Serving: Where and Why to Serve 72
   Defensive Plays: Keeping the Ball in Your
   Court 75
   Offensive Strategies: Taking Control of
   the Game 80
   Mastering the Lob and Smash 84
   Doubles Strategy: Working Effectively with
   Your Partner 87

5. OVERCOMING COMMON CHALLENGES 93
   Navigating the Non-Volley Zone: Techniques
   and Tactics 93
   Handling High-Pressure Situations in
   Match Play 96
   Overcoming Plateaus: Tips for Continued
   Improvement 99
   Dealing with Adverse Weather Conditions 102
   Equipment Malfunctions and On-the-Fly Fixes 106
   Common Rule Misunderstandings and How to
   Clarify Them 108

6. PRACTICE MAKES PERFECT 113
   Solo Drills for Skill Enhancement 113
   Partner Drills to Enhance Coordination and
   Reflexes 116
   Team Practices: Engaging Group Drills 119
   Using Technology: Apps and Tools for Better
   Practice 122
   Creating a Personal Practice Schedule 125
   Measuring Progress: Tracking Skills and
   Improvement 127

7. THE SOCIAL AND COMMUNITY ASPECT OF
   PICKLEBALL 131
   Finding and Joining Pickleball Clubs and
   Leagues 132
   Hosting Pickleball Events and Tournaments 135

Building a Pickleball Community: Tips and
Strategies 138
Pickleball for All Ages: Engaging Different
Generations 141
The Role of Social Media in Growing Your
Pickleball Network 147

8. TAKING YOUR GAME TO THE NEXT LEVEL 151
Preparing for Your First Tournament 152
Advanced Competitive Strategies 154
Mental Toughness in Competitive Play 156
Nutrition and Fitness for Peak Performance 158
The Etiquette of Competitive Pickleball 162
Reflecting on Your Pickleball Journey: Growth
and Goals 165

Conclusion 171
References 175

INTRODUCTION

You've probably heard that pickleball is the fastest-growing sport in the world. And for good reason! I fell in love with this sport the first time I stepped onto the court. There I was, standing on what looked like a shrunken tennis court, surrounded by players who seemed to dance around with ease. I felt a mix of confusion and intrigue as the ball whizzed back and forth. My bafflement quickly blossomed into a full-blown passion. I want to take you on this journey from novice to enthusiast, just as I went through it.

This book is crafted with a clear purpose: to demystify the game of pickleball for you, whether you're just starting out or seeking to sharpen your skills. I have been playing professional pickleball for over a decade, and I believe I am the perfect person to help you get the best out of this game.

You could be reading this book for a range of reasons. Maybe you're overwhelmed by the sport's growing popularity and struggling to find a comprehensive guide to the game. Maybe you're trying to pick the sport up after playing tennis or badminton and struggling to transition smoothly to the new rules. Maybe you are eager to engage in pickleball's social community but don't want to feel left out because of your lack of skill. Maybe you've been playing pickleball for a while, but you've noticed a plateau in your ability and don't know how to improve. Or maybe you've just picked this book up on a whim, looking for a new, fun, and active way to spend time with your family. Whatever your reason, I guarantee that this book will help you.

Pickleball is a sport for everyone. It doesn't matter if you're a teenager looking for a new challenge, an adult seeking a fun way to stay active, or an athlete trying to expand your skills. This book is designed to be your companion, guiding you through each stage of your pickleball journey.

In chapter one, we'll cover the origins and history of pickleball. This will include an explanation of the basic pickleball gear and court layout, and go over the rules of the game and some essential pickleball terminology.

In chapter two, we look at how you can physically prepare to play. Here, we provide a guide to warming up and cooling down with the best stretches. This chapter will discuss how to build your physical ability through endurance, strength, flexibility, and agility training. And, it will explain how to sharpen your mind before you play with focus techniques.

In chapter three, we cover all the basic techniques of pickleball. This includes the serve, the return, the volley, the dink, the backhand, and footwork.

In chapter four, we move on to advanced skills and strategies. This chapter will explore strategic serving and targeting weaknesses on the court. Then, we explain the best ways to play defensively and offensively.

In chapter five, we tackle some common challenges in pickleball. In this chapter, we'll teach you to navigate the non-volley zone like a pro. We cover handling the high-pressure of competitive games and provide a guide to overcoming plateaus and ensuring your continued skill improvement. We look at different adverse weather conditions, including heat, wind, and cold, and how you should adjust your play accordingly. You will learn some quick fixes to deal with any equipment malfunctions. Finally, we clarify some common rule misunderstandings.

In chapter six, we explain all of the best ways you can practice improving your pickleball. This chapter includes detailed drills for solo work, partner work, and teamwork, with a look at how you can use technology to practice better. Finally, we explain the best way to create your own training schedule and how you can measure your progress over time.

In chapter seven, we look at the community aspect of pickleball. This chapter will explain how you can find the best club in your area that is suited to your needs. We cover how pickleball is a sport for any age, and talk about youth engagement, senior engagement, and family-friendly fun. We also explore how social media can be used to expand your pickleball network.

In chapter eight, we cover how you can take your game to the next level by competing in tournaments. In this chapter, you will receive preparation advice, tactical game day strategies, and nutrition and fitness advice suited for the more serious players. You will also learn proper pickleball etiquette, to help you avoid making any blunders on your game day.

As you turn these pages, I encourage you to not just read but engage. Practice the drills, reflect on the strategies, and perhaps most importantly, connect with the pickleball community around you. This is where the true joy and growth in pickleball lie.

Writing this book has deepened my appreciation for pickleball and its community. I've gathered insights, strategies, and stories that I hope will not only inform you but also inspire a deep, lasting love for the game. Let's step onto the court together, with paddle in hand, ready to play, learn, and connect.

Welcome to the wonderful world of pickleball.

THE ORIGINS AND ESSENTIALS OF PICKLEBALL

This chapter will provide you with all the fundamentals of pickleball. To start, we'll explain how pickleball grew from a makeshift family game into a global sport. From here, we provide a comprehensive overview to choose the best pickleball gear. We explain how to find yourself a paddle based on its core, surface material, shape, and weight, and explain the difference between indoor and outdoor balls. From here, we'll break down the pickleball court layout and its different court surfaces.

Next, we provide a simple overview of the rules to get you started—from serving to the two-bounce rule to faults like the no-volley zone. To wrap up, we provide a short glossary of some key pickleball terms to help you get a grasp of the game. Finally, we have a simple step-by-step guide to set you up for your first game.

TRACING THE LINES: THE BIRTH AND SPREAD OF PICKLEBALL

Historical Context

In the summer of 1965 on Bainbridge Island, Washington, two friends invented pickleball. Joel Pritchard, a congressman, and Bill Bell, a successful businessman, returned from a game of golf to find their children bored at Prichard's home. They sought to entertain their kids through a game of badminton on an old court, but they couldn't find all the equipment. So, they improvised and began to play the game with some old table tennis paddles and a perforated plastic ball. As they played, they saw that the ball bounced well on the court, leading them to lower the badminton net to 36 inches high. The following weekend, their friend Barney McCallum joined them, and together, the three men developed the rules for their new game. In their aim to entertain their bored families one summer afternoon, the men unknowingly gave birth to a new sport—pickleball (Onix Pickleball n.d.).

There's some debate as to how this new sport got its name. Neighbors of the Pritchards claimed that the game was named after the Pritchards' family dog, Pickles, who would chase after the errant balls. However, the Pritchard family insisted that they got the dog years later and named him after the game. Rather, the name *pickleball* was drawn from a reference to the "pickle boats" of local crew races, where the oarsmen were picked from the leftovers of other boats. The combination of different sports that went into pickleball reminded Joan Pritchard of these motley crews (USAP n.d.-a).

The Evolution of the Game

From these informal beginnings on Bainbridge Island, pickleball began to take shape into a more structured sport. The original rules were established by 1967 to standardize play, primarily to maintain fairness and competitiveness among players. As more people were introduced to the game, its popularity grew, spreading first through Pritchard's connections in Washington and then across the United States. In 1967, the first permanent pickleball court was built in the backyard of Pritchard's friend and neighbor, Bob O'Brian. Schools, community centers, and local sports facilities started to adopt pickleball, drawn by its easy-to-learn nature and minimal equipment needs, making it accessible and enjoyable for all ages.

By 1976, the first known pickleball tournament was held in Tukwila, Washington, signaling a shift from a backyard family activity to a more serious sport. At this point, many of the participants were college tennis players who knew very little about pickleball. However, this event paved the way for structured competitive play and helped in formulating standardized rules and equipment specifications, which were essential as the sport gained a formal competitive edge.

One of the most significant milestones in pickleball history was the establishment of the USA Pickleball Association in 1984, later renamed USA Pickleball (USAP) in 2020. The USAP was formed to promote the growth of the sport on a national level. USAP published the first rulebook in March of 1984, creating the necessary formalization for pickleball's acceptance as a legitimate sport. By 1990, pickleball was being played in all 50 US states.

Further recognition came as pickleball was included in the 2001 Arizona Senior Olympic games, drawing over 100 players, the largest pickleball ever played to that point. In 2009, pickleball was included for the first time at the National Senior Games Association. These developments not only affirmed pickleball's status as an established sport but also helped in expanding its reach to more players globally.

As pickleball continued to grow, so did the methods by which people learned about and engaged with the sport. The advent of the internet and social media played a pivotal role in spreading awareness about pickleball. Social media platforms have become a hub for players to connect with one another, share tips, and promote pickleball tournaments. These digital tools have not only made learning about pickleball more accessible but have also helped players from different parts of the world connect over their shared love for the game, with pickleball courts popping up all over the world, from Canada to Europe to Asia, echoing the game's universal appeal and adaptability (Fairgrounds 2023).

In 2021, USA Pickleball Membership grew 43% to reach 53,000 members, the fastest growth year to date for the organization. The Sports and Fitness Industry Association has now named pickleball the fastest-growing sport in America for three consecutive years. Their 2023 report estimates that there are over 8.9 million players and 11,000 locations to play in the US (USAP n.d.-a). According to the 2023

APP Pickleball Participation Report, numbers are even higher, with 36.5 million Americans playing pickleball in the last year (The Dink Media Team 2023b).

The simplicity and accessibility of pickleball have been critical to its widespread adoption. It is a game that can be played by anyone, regardless of age or athletic ability, which has contributed significantly to its growth. Families can play it together, friends can form leagues, and communities can hold tournaments. This inclusive nature has not only helped pickleball spread geographically but has also enabled it to build a strong and inclusive community. Clearly, this sport is here to stay.

CHOOSING YOUR GEAR: A COMPREHENSIVE GUIDE TO PICKLEBALL EQUIPMENT

Selecting the right equipment is pivotal in any sport, and pickleball is no exception. The gear you choose affects not only your performance but also your enjoyment of the game. While many pickleball venues will have equipment that you can hire on-site, you will likely want to buy some for yourself if you're playing more regularly.

The Paddle

It's essential to start with the right paddle, the primary tool of the game. The paddle is made up of a handle and a large flat surface, which is used to hit the ball over the net. When choosing a pickleball paddle, you should consider the core, the surface material, the shape, and the weight.

Almost all pickleball paddles will have a polymer core, whether they're $20 or $200. The higher-priced paddles use a better-quality polymer core that doesn't break down as easily. More important to consider than material is the thickness of the core.

- Thicker cores (around 16 mm) stabilize the paddle and increase control. This thickness is highly recommended for a beginner.
- Thinner cores (between 10 mm and 14 mm) are less stable but can produce more power. If you're an aggressive player who likes to attack the ball, you might prefer a thinner core.

Pickleball paddles come in a variety of surface materials, which can influence your power, accuracy, and control. There are three main materials used for the surface of the paddle: fiberglass, carbon fiber, and graphite.

- Fiberglass (composite) paddles used to be most common in pickleball. The material is not very stiff, so the paddle acts as a trampoline to transfer the energy of the ball back out. This gives the paddle a lot of power.
- Carbon fiber is now the most popular material for pickleball paddles. It is a stiff and durable material, so the energy of the ball at impact is spread throughout the paddle. This loses some power but gives you a much better feel for accuracy and control.

- Graphite is a type of carbon fiber and plays very similarly to a carbon fiber paddle. This type of paddle is known for offering the best responsiveness, accuracy, and control.

Another thing to consider is the shape of the paddle:

- An elongated shape will give you more reach, power, and spin, but has less maneuverability.
- A widebody shape will give you more control and maneuverability but has less reach and power.
- A classic shape offers a balanced mix of power, spin, control, and maneuverability.

Finally, when choosing a paddle, consider the weight that feels most comfortable for you.

- **Heavier paddles offer more power.** You don't have to swing as hard because there is weight behind the ball. They are also more stable, reducing the room for error. However, a heavier paddle may lead to faster arm fatigue, making lighter paddles preferable for longer play sessions or for players with limited upper body strength.
- **Lighter paddles are easier to maneuver, giving you an advantage in fast exchanges.** However, you need to swing harder to get more power out of it. Many players add lead tape to the edge of their lighter paddles to make them heavier (Unsicker 2022).

Popular brands like Selkirk, Paddletek, and Onix offer models that cater to a range of preferences and skill levels, and many sporting goods stores allow you to test different paddles before making a purchase, ensuring you find the perfect fit for your hand and play style.

The Ball

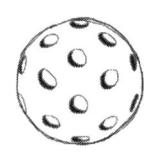

The ball used in pickleball also varies, depending on whether you play indoors or outdoors. The ball is made of plastic, completely hollow, and covered in holes. Indoor balls are typically softer and lighter, designed to perform well on smooth, flat surfaces. They have 26 large holes and less weight, which allows for better control and slower play. Outdoor balls, on the other hand, are made to endure rougher, textured court surfaces like concrete. They're harder, heavier, and have 40 smaller, more tightly spaced holes. This design helps reduce the effects of wind and produces a faster, more challenging game. When choosing a ball, consider where most of your games will be played and select a ball that's designed for that environment to ensure the best performance and durability.

Your Clothing

You don't need any fancy gear to play pickleball. You can wear any sportswear or comfy clothes that won't restrict your movement. If you're playing outdoors for an extended period, a lightweight long-sleeved top can provide good sun protection. Opt for sneakers that provide good support and traction to handle the quick lateral movements that pickleball requires. Court shoes designed for tennis or volleyball

THE ORIGINS AND ESSENTIALS OF PICKLEBALL | 19

make excellent choices, as they offer the necessary lateral support and have soles suited for the kind of quick, sharp movements typical in pickleball.

Additional Gear

More serious players can seek out additional gear such as bags, grips, and protective eyewear to enhance their pickleball experience. A good quality bag can organize and protect your equipment, with specialized compartments for paddles, balls, and personal items. Grips help absorb sweat and improve handle feel, which can enhance control and reduce the risk of slipping during play. For those who play frequently or competitively, investing in high-quality grips and regularly replacing them can significantly improve play comfort and effectiveness. Protective eyewear can be used by players at all levels to protect against accidental impacts from balls or paddles. Safety glasses designed specifically for racquet sports can offer UV protection for outdoor play.

Each piece of equipment in pickleball serves a purpose and choosing the right items can enhance your performance and enjoyment of the game. Whether you're just starting out or looking to upgrade your current gear, taking the time to select equipment that fits your needs and playing style is an important step in your pickleball progression.

UNDERSTANDING PICKLEBALL COURTS: LAYOUT AND SPECIFICATIONS

A standard pickleball court measures 20 feet in width and 44 feet in length, inclusive of lines, which are similar in layout to a badminton court (VMKMON Sport n.d.). These dimensions are used for both singles and doubles play. The net splits the court into two equal halves, with a height of 36 inches at the sidelines and slightly lower at the center, standing at 34 inches. This slight height difference helps prevent the ball from rolling off the net when it is hit.

The service areas are 10 feet wide and 15 feet long and are divided by the non-volley zone, also known as the "kitchen," which extends seven feet from the net on either side. This zone is a crucial area in pickleball, as players are not allowed to volley the ball within this zone, thus preventing them from executing smashes right at the net and maintaining a fair play dynamic.

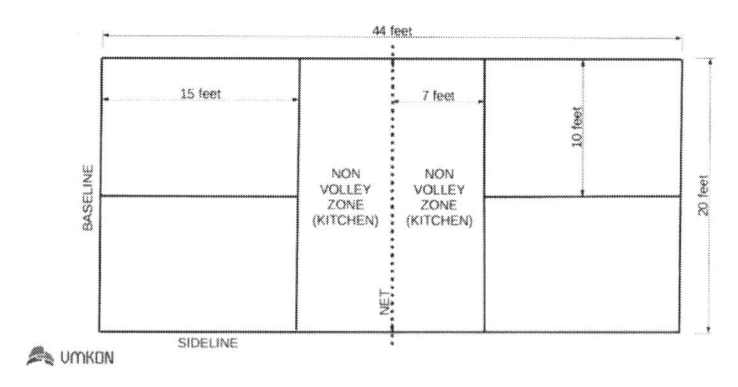

Pickleball Court Dimensions, VMKON Sport, https://vmkonsport.com/pickleball-court-dimensions

Court Surface Materials

The surface of a pickleball court can significantly affect gameplay. Like tennis, common pickleball court materials include concrete and asphalt, although grass and clay surfaces are trending. Each surface type presents its own set of advantages and challenges, influencing ball bounce, speed, and player comfort. Concrete provides a hard, stable base and is favored for its durability and low maintenance. However, it can be tough on joints during prolonged play. Asphalt is another popular choice, offering slightly more cushioning than concrete. It does require more maintenance to fill cracks and smooth out uneven areas that develop over time. Pickleball players have recently begun branching away from the traditional surfaces to clay or grass. These surfaces create a more unpredictable bounce, adding variety to the game (Paddletek n.d.-c).

Setting up Temporary Courts

For those who do not have access to permanent pickleball facilities, setting up a temporary court is easy enough. You can play pickleball in a gymnasium, community center, or your own driveway, as long as there is a flat surface large enough to accommodate the court dimensions. To set up a temporary court, you'll need portable net systems that can easily be set up and taken down. Use painter's tape or temporary chalk to mark the boundaries and non-volley zones. Ensure the playing surface is clean and flat to prevent injuries and ensure consistent ball play. Temporary courts are an excellent way for communities and schools to introduce pickleball to participants without the need for permanent installations. As pickleball continues to grow in popularity, the adaptability and simplicity of setting up courts play a significant role in making the sport accessible to everyone, everywhere.

THE RULES OF THE GAME: AN EASY GUIDE FOR BEGINNERS

When you step onto a pickleball court, whether as a newcomer to the sport or a seasoned player looking to refine your understanding of the rules, it's crucial to grasp the foundational components that govern the game. This understanding not only enhances your ability to play effectively but also ensures that the game is played fairly and enjoyably by all participants. Let's break down these rules.

Serving Rules

The serve in pickleball is distinctively different from many other racquet sports. It must be executed underhand, meaning the server's arm is moving in an upward arc, and the paddle must make contact with the ball below the waist level. The server's feet must be behind the baseline during the serve. The first serve is made from the right court. It is hit diagonally crosscourt, so the ball must land in the opposite diagonal box beyond the non-volley zone, commonly referred to as the kitchen. If the server wins the point, they move to the left-hand side and continue to alternate sides with each point won while retaining the serve. Should the server lose a point, the serve passes to the opponent.

In doubles, the sequence becomes slightly more complex as the serve alternates between partners each time they win a point until a fault leads to a serve change. However, at the beginning of each game, only one partner of the serving team can serve before faulting, after which the serve passes to the receiving team. In subsequent plays, the second server continues serving until their team commits a fault and loses the serve. An ideal serve sets the tone for the rally, aiming to be low enough to make it difficult for the opponent to execute a powerful return. Practicing different serving techniques, such as the soft serve or the power serve, can significantly impact your game strategy, giving you an edge by varying your serve style to keep opponents guessing.

Two-Bounce Rule

The flow of a standard pickleball game starts with the serve, followed by a return from the opponent. One of the unique aspects of pickleball is the two-bounce rule, which mandates that each side must let the ball bounce once before volleys are allowed. This rule applies to the first return by the receiving side and the subsequent return by the serving side. After these two bounces, players may then choose to volley the ball (hit the ball before it bounces) or play it off a bounce (ground stroke) during the rally. This rule is designed to extend rallies and create a more strategic game.

In doubles play, communication and coordination with your partner become crucial. Effective strategies often involve one player managing the baseline while the other positions closer to the net, ready to volley. The synergy between partners can significantly control the pace and style of the game, making doubles an exciting and dynamic version of pickleball.

Faults

A fault is any action that stops play because of a rule violation. A fault by the serving team will result in the loss of serve, while a fault by the receiving team will result in a point for the serving team. Common faults include a foot fault, where a player steps on or over the baseline while serving, or into the non-volley zone on a volley shot. Another frequent fault is failing to clear the net or hitting the ball out of bounds. Additionally, volleying the ball in the non-volley zone, the space that extends seven feet from the net, is a specific rule designed to prevent players from executing smashes from a position too close to the net (Paddletek n.d.-a). It is a fault even if the player is driven by momentum after volleying to touch the non-volley zone (the kitchen). Each of these faults can quickly turn the tide of a game, making it essential for players to cultivate precision and awareness in their play to minimize these errors.

Basic Scoring

In pickleball, points can only be scored by the serving side, which adds a strategic layer to serving. Each game is typically played to 11 points, and a team must win by at least a two-point margin. Tournament games may be played to 15 or 21 points (USAP 2023).

Score Calling

The score should always be called before serving, starting with the serving team's score, then the receiving team's score, and in doubles, ending with the server number (either one or two, depending on whether they are the first or second server for their team). For example, if the serving team has four points, the receiving team has three, and the server is the first server of their team, the call would be 4-3-1. This method keeps everyone on the court aware of the game status and who is serving, which can influence play strategy and positioning.

As you continue to play and familiarize yourself with these rules, you'll find that your strategic choices and your enjoyment of the game deepen. Each rule and regulation is designed not merely as a limitation but as a way to enhance the challenge and the pleasure of pickleball. Whether you're serving, volleying, or strategically positioning yourself on the court, a clear understanding of these guidelines assures not just correct play, but also a fair and competitive environment for everyone involved.

ESSENTIAL PICKLEBALL TERMINOLOGY: SLANG AND LINGO DECODED

When you first step onto a pickleball court, you might feel like you're learning a new language. Terms like "dink" and "volley" fly around just as much as the ball does. Let's break down some of these key terms and common slang, which will not only help you understand the game better but also make you sound like a seasoned player.

- **Dink:** A soft shot in pickleball, made from near the net, intended to drop into the opponent's non-volley zone, the kitchen. The strategy behind a dink is to make it difficult for the opponent to return it with power, often leading to a more advantageous position or an outright point. The term itself might sound playful, but mastering the dink is a skill that can significantly elevate your game. It's a finesse shot that requires precision and control, contrasting sharply with the more aggressive "smash" or "drive" shots that shoot the ball across the court with high velocity.

- **Volley:** Much like in tennis, this refers to hitting the ball before it bounces. In the context of pickleball, this is typically done near the net but outside of the non-volley zone. This technique is crucial for aggressive play and can help keep opponents on their back foot. However, it requires good timing and positioning to execute effectively, as hitting a volley from a poor stance or at an inopportune moment can easily send the ball into the net or out of bounds.
- **Rally:** It is the sequence of hitting the ball back and forth between players or teams, starting from the serve and continuing until a point is scored or a fault is made. Rallies can be short and sharp, with powerful drives, or long and strategic, featuring a mix of dinks and volleys. They are the essence of pickleball gameplay, where both the physical skills and strategic thinking of the players are put to the test.
- **Poach:** It is a term used when a player crosses over the centerline to play a ball that might ordinarily be played by their partner in doubles. This move can be great as it can save the point if executed correctly and catch opponents off guard. Poaching requires a high level of teamwork and understanding between

partners, as it disrupts positioning, making it a risky yet potentially rewarding strategy.
- **Pickle:** It is a fun exclamation sometimes used when a particularly good or unexpected shot is made, deriving from the name of the sport itself.
- **Kitchen:** As previously discussed, it refers to the non-volley zone, a seven-foot area extending from the net on both sides of the court. This area is a critical part of the game strategy in pickleball, where players can legally enter the zone at any time but cannot hit a ball out of the air in this zone.

Of course, courts may develop their own slang and terminology. Don't be afraid to ask someone what they mean when they yell out a term!

Communication Cues in Doubles

In doubles play, communication between partners is key to coordinating movements and shots, ensuring both players are positioned optimally and aware of game tactics. Verbal cues are commonly used to indicate who should take the ball or what kind of shot to play. Phrases like "yours" or "mine" quickly tell a partner to leave a ball or take it. More advanced players might use specific calls like "switch" or "stay" to direct court positioning during play, or even call out planned shots like "dink" or "drive" to set up strategic plays. Effective communication not only helps prevent collisions and missed shots but also strengthens the partnership, making the team more cohesive and difficult to beat.

Understanding and using these terms and cues effectively can transform how you play and experience pickleball. They allow you to communicate succinctly, plan strategically, and engage fully with the community and the culture of the sport. As you continue to play and interact with other players, these elements of language will become second nature, enhancing your enjoyment and mastery of the game.

SETTING UP YOUR FIRST GAME: A STEP-BY-STEP GUIDE

Embarking on your first game of pickleball comes with its share of excitement and a bit of preparation to ensure everything goes smoothly.

1. **Select the right venue.** Ideally, look for a location that has a proper pickleball court, like public parks, community centers, and local sports clubs. When choosing a venue, consider the surface of the court, as different materials can affect how the game plays out. Also, consider the availability of the courts, as some places might require a reservation, especially during peak times. Lastly, consider the community aspect. Some venues have a more competitive atmosphere, while others are more recreational. Choose a place where you will feel comfortable, especially for your first few games.
2. **Prepare your equipment.** This includes ensuring you have the right paddle to match your playing style and balls that are appropriate for the court type—indoor or outdoor. Dress appropriately for physical activity, wearing comfortable sports clothes and

shoes designed for court sports to avoid slips and falls. It's also wise to pack water and snacks, especially if you're playing multiple games or during hot weather, to stay hydrated and energized. A small sports bag can keep all your gear organized and ready to go.
3. **Warm up to prepare your body for the activity ahead.** Begin with a general warm-up to raise your heart rate, like jogging lightly or doing jumping jacks for a few minutes. Follow this with dynamic stretches focusing on your arms, legs, and back to ensure full mobility during the game. Include movements that mimic pickleball actions, such as side lunges, arm circles, and gentle paddle swings. If possible, engage in a light rally with your opponent or a friend to get a feel for the ball and the paddle before the actual game begins. This not only warms you up but also helps in reducing the initial nervousness of playing. We'll explore warming up in more detail in chapter two.
4. **Be respectful and have fun.** Sportsmanship is paramount; always respect your opponent, the officials, and the rules of the game. Calls should be made honestly, and disputes should be handled calmly. If a disagreement arises, try to resolve it politely and continue the game with a focus on enjoyment rather than contention. Remember, the primary goal of your first game is to learn and have fun. Celebrate good shots by your opponent and yourself, and don't dwell on mistakes. Encourage a positive atmosphere and enjoy the social interaction that comes with playing pickleball.

As you step onto the court for your first game, remember that every player starts somewhere, and every expert was once a beginner. Take this initial experience as a learning opportunity and a chance to enjoy a new activity. With an open and willing mindset, your first game of pickleball can be the beginning of a long and joyful hobby with a sport that is loved by many for its fun, social, and competitive nature. So, grab your paddle, step on the court, and get ready to enjoy the game!

PREPARING TO PLAY: PHYSICAL AND MENTAL READINESS

Stepping onto the pickleball court isn't just about having the right paddle in hand or understanding the rules of the game. Equally important is ensuring that your body and mind are prepped and primed for the fun of pickleball. This chapter is dedicated to getting you ready, not just to play, but to excel and enjoy every moment of your pickleball experience, from the first serve to the final point.

We'll begin with a fundamental aspect that many beginners overlook: the importance of proper warm-ups and cool-downs. These are not just routine stretches and exercises; they are your first steps toward injury prevention and better performance on the court. Next, we discuss how to focus your mind and handle pressure so that you play your best game possible. From here, we'll look at some cross-training that you can do to improve your pickleball skills. Finally, we give some final tips to prevent any injuries while you play.

WARM-UPS AND COOL-DOWNS: ESSENTIAL EXERCISES FOR PICKLEBALL

Dynamic Stretching

Before you even think about hitting the court, it's crucial to get your muscles and joints ready for the action. Dynamic stretching is ideal for this. Unlike static stretching, which involves holding a stretch for a long period, dynamic stretches are active movements where joints and muscles go through a full range of motion. They help increase blood flow, warm up your muscles, and improve your range of motion before exercise. Studies suggest that dynamic stretching before playing sports decreases the risk of injury (Chertoff 2019). Here are a few key dynamic stretches:

- **Leg Swings:** Hold onto a back fence or a sturdy object for balance, and gently swing one leg forward and backward, gradually increasing the range of motion. This exercise loosens up your hamstrings and hip flexors, key players in those quick, sudden movements you'll be making during the game.
- **Leg Circles:** Stand on one leg, holding onto a fence or wall for support. Gently swing your other leg in small circles out to the side, gradually working up to larger circles. Perform 20 circles and then switch legs.
- **Arm Circles:** Extend your arms straight out to your sides and make slow, controlled circles, gradually increasing the diameter of the circles. This motion

prepares your upper body for all the arm action needed in serving and volleying.

- **Torso Twists:** To warm up your core and lower back, stand with your feet hip-width apart and your knees slightly bent, then twist your torso to the right and left, letting your arms swing loosely. This helps engage your core, which is essential for balance and power during play.
- **Lunge with a Twist:** Lunge forward on your right leg, keeping your knee directly over your ankle and not extending it further. Reach overhead with your left arm and bend your torso to the right side. Bring your leg back to an upright position, then repeat on the opposite side. This movement prepares your lower body to move forward, stop, and then reverse directions. Adding the rotation to the movement prepares your core muscles and spine for swings to hit the ball.

Sport-Specific Drills

Once your muscles are warmed up, move on to drills that mimic the specific movements of pickleball.

- **Light Jogging:** Run slowly around the pickleball court. This will gently raise your temperature, increase your circulation, and awaken your joints and muscles.
- **Lateral Shuffles:** These are excellent for improving your side-to-side court movement. Start on one side of the pickleball court, squat slightly, and shuffle your feet quickly to the other side, then shuffle back.

This drill enhances your agility and mimics the quick lateral movements required during a game.
- **Forward Sprints:** Incorporating quick forward sprints can improve your ability to rush toward the net or retreat back to the baseline. Start at the center of the court, sprint forward to the net, touch it, then quickly backpedal to the baseline. Repeat several times. This drill helps improve your speed and footwork, which is crucial for getting in the best position to hit the ball effectively.

The Importance of Cool-Downs

After the game, it's just as important to cool down as it was to warm up. Cooling down helps your body transition back to a normal resting state and can significantly reduce muscle stiffness and soreness. While we wanted to avoid static stretching for warming up, cooling down is the perfect time to implement it. Stretching can make a difference in how well your muscles recover after exercise. When static stretching, we want to stretch a specific muscle to the point where it feels slightly uncomfortable and hold that position for 15-45 seconds. Begin your cool-down with gentle stretching focusing on the major muscle groups used in pickleball—the legs, arms, and back. This will help to relax your muscles, increase your flexibility over time, lessen any pain or stiffness, and increase your performance when you next play (Cronkleton 2019).

Make sure that you're stretching safely. The stretch should be slightly uncomfortable, but not painful. Stop right away if you feel sharp pain. Use slow, gentle movements and avoid jerking your muscles into place. Make sure you take slow, deep breaths as you stretch. This will help relieve tension from your body and can help you hold the stretch for longer. Here are a few static stretches:

- **Standing Hamstring Stretch:** Extend one leg out so that it is resting on your heel, with the toe pointing up. Keeping the spine straight, bend at the hip to bring the chest toward the thigh. Gently reach your hands down your leg toward the front foot. Hold for 30 seconds, then repeat on the other leg.
- **Standing Quadriceps Stretch:** Hold onto a wall or fence for balance. Bend one leg by holding your ankle in your hand and pulling your foot back to your buttocks. Gently pull on the ankle to bend your knee and feel the stretch through your quad. If you can't feel the stretch, tuck your hips forward. Maintain for 30 seconds and then swap legs.
- **Cross-Body Shoulder Stretch:** In a standing position, take one arm and place it across your chest. Use your other arm to push that arm into your body and feel more of a stretch. Make sure that your elbow remains at shoulder height. Hold for 30 seconds and then repeat on the other arm.
- **Chest Opener Stretch:** Clasp your hands behind your back. Squeeze your shoulder blades together to stretch out the chest muscles. For some additional stretch, lift your hands upwards off your back.
- **Side Stretch:** Stand with your feet shoulder-width apart. Raise one arm over your head, and then lean to the side. Slide your relaxed arm down the side of your leg to deepen the stretch. Hold for 30 seconds

and then repeat on the other side. This will stretch your core and back.

Routine Examples

For a complete warm-up, perform each dynamic stretch for about 30 seconds to one minute and each drill for about two to three minutes. Ensure you're gradually increasing the intensity to safely raise your heart rate and muscle temperature. Here's a quick 10-minute routine you can follow before playing:

1. Leg swings (30 seconds each leg)
2. Arm circles (30 seconds each arm, both directions)
3. Torso twists (one minute)
4. Lateral shuffles (two minutes)
5. Quick forward sprints (two minutes)

For cooling down, spend about five minutes doing the following static stretches:

1. Hamstring stretch (30 seconds each leg)
2. Quadriceps stretch (30 seconds each leg)
3. Cross-body shoulder stretch (30 seconds each arm)
4. Chest opener (30 seconds)
5. Side stretch (30 seconds each side)

By incorporating these warm-up and cool-down routines into your pickleball sessions, you not only enhance your performance but also significantly decrease your risk of injury, ensuring that every game is as enjoyable as possible. Remember, a well-prepared player is a player set up for success, enjoyment, and continual improvement in the exciting world of pickleball.

PHYSICAL ABILITY: BUILDING ENDURANCE, STRENGTH, FLEXIBILITY, AND AGILITY FOR BETTER PLAY

Pickleball, while fun and engaging, demands not just skill with the paddle but also considerable physical endurance, muscle strength, flexibility, and agility. If you're concerned about keeping up with the fast-paced nature of the game, you can develop these physical attributes. Endurance allows you to maintain your energy levels throughout a long match or a tournament day, strength allows your body to handle the repetitive movements, agility helps you make those quick, sharp plays that can often be the difference between winning and losing a point, and flexibility allows you to move around without injuring yourself.

Endurance

Endurance refers to your body's physical capability to sustain an exercise for an extended period. It is made up of two parts: cardiovascular endurance, the heart's ability to fuel the lungs and body with oxygen, and muscular endurance, the ability of the muscles to work continuously. It's important to engage in activities that engage your muscles, elevate your heart rate, and improve your cardiovascular health. The American Heart Association recommends a minimum of 150 minutes of aerobic exercise per week but getting over 300 minutes has additional benefits (Yetman 2020).

- **Jogging is a straightforward and effective way to build endurance.** It doesn't require much equipment, and you can vary your pace and distance to continually challenge yourself. If this is too much pressure on your joints, try a brisk walk up some hills.
- **Cycling, whether on a stationary bike or outdoors, is another excellent cardiovascular exercise.** It has the added benefit of being low-impact, which reduces stress on your joints while still providing a great workout for your heart and lungs.
- **Interval training, or HIIT, is particularly effective for pickleball players.** It involves alternating short bursts of intense activity with periods of rest or lower-intensity activity. This type of training mimics the stop-start nature of the game, helping improve your recovery time and ability to sustain effort during long rallies. Try doing a round of 10-second sprints with a 30-second rest between each sprint.

Make sure that you make gradual increases in either the volume or intensity of your exercise to continue improving your fitness. For example, if you choose to jog to build your endurance, make sure that each week you slightly increase either the distance, the speed, or the amount of time you run.

Strength Training

One crucial component of a balanced training regimen is strength training, which focuses on building the muscles you rely on most during play. Strength is defined as the ability to produce maximal force against a specific resistance. Strength is an integral part of health and is linked to decreases in mortality causes. By strengthening your core, legs, and arms, you not only increase your power and stability but also ensure that your body can handle the quick, repetitive movements required in pickleball without succumbing to fatigue (Edwards 2022).

Strength training exercises tailored for pickleball should target the major muscle groups used during the game.

- **Core Strength:** For the core, exercises like planks, Russian twists, and bicycle crunches help improve your stability and ability to rotate your body efficiently, which is essential for powerful swings.
- **Leg Strength:** Leg exercises such as squats, lunges, and calf raises build the lower body strength necessary for quick sprints and sustained agility on the court.
- **Arm Strength:** For arm strength, incorporate exercises like push-ups, tricep dips, and bicep curls, which enhance your ability to hit the ball with force and precision.

It's important to balance these exercises with appropriate rest periods to allow muscles to recover and grow stronger. Aim to integrate strength training into your routine two to three times per week, focusing on different muscle groups each session to prevent overtraining. To improve your strength over time, you need to make gradual increases in the weight you're lifting, the number of repetitions you do, or the number of days you strength train.

Flexibility

Flexibility refers to the ability to move our muscles and joints through a full range of motion. In addition to strength training, maintaining flexibility is vital for preventing injuries and ensuring that your body can move freely and fluidly during a game. Here are a few ways to improve your flexibility:

- **Perform dynamic stretching prior to an activity.** As you move back and forth through your joint's range of motion, you gradually increase your flexibility.
- **Perform static stretching after an activity.** Your muscles are warm and pliable after working out, so you can extend your muscles further during this time.
- **Try out yoga or Pilates.** These practices involve a series of poses and stretches that elongate the muscles, improve balance, and enhance breathing control. Yoga, with its emphasis on stretching and relaxation, can particularly help in loosening tight muscles and improving range of motion. Pilates focuses more on core strength, which is indispensable for maintaining proper posture and power in pickleball. Engaging in yoga or Pilates sessions a few times a week can significantly enhance your flexibility, reduce the risk of muscle strains, and support overall body alignment.

Agility

Agility is our ability to safely slow down, change directions, and speed up in as little time as possible. Apart from improving your ability to move around quickly on the pickleball court, agility training also improves your strength, explosive power, balance, and mobility. Agility training involves drills that require quick changes of direction and train your body to move more swiftly and efficiently on the court (Read 2021).

- **Cone Side Shuffle:** Place two cones or markers roughly 15 steps apart. Imagine a perpendicular line between the cones that you will travel along. Bend your knees slightly into a quarter squat. Without crossing your feet, step sideways toward the far cone in a side shuffle. When you reach the far cone, stop, and accelerate in the opposite direction. Add speed and intensity as you warm up.
- **Cone Grapevine:** Place two cones or markers roughly 15 steps apart. Imagine a perpendicular line between the cones that you will travel along. Bend your knees slightly into a quarter squat. Move sideways between the cones in a grapevine pattern, so that your leg crosses first behind and then in front of your leading leg. When you reach the far cone, stop, and accelerate in the opposite direction. Add speed and intensity as you warm up.
- **Ladder Runs:** There are a variety of agility exercises you can do with an agility ladder. Try the two-in-one linear run, where you move forward up the ladder, stepping your leading foot into the box, and then

bringing your other foot next to it. Continue down the ladder using the same leading foot. Repeat the drill with the opposite foot as the leading foot.

As you continue to develop your physical capabilities through these targeted exercises, you'll find that your ability to handle the rigors of intense play improves markedly. Not only will you see a difference in your capacity to manage back-to-back games or long rally sessions, but your improved agility will also allow you to reach shots quicker and with more balance, giving you the edge you need to compete at higher levels and enjoy every moment on the court.

Monitoring your progress is key to understanding how well your training aligns with your performance goals. Use tools and apps designed for tracking physical fitness to keep tabs on your activities. Many of these tools can monitor your heart rate, calculate calories burned, and even provide insights into recovery times and progress trends. They can be particularly helpful for setting benchmarks and recognizing when adjustments need to be made in your training regimen. By consistently measuring your performance, you can make informed decisions about how to adjust your workouts to better meet the demands of pickleball, ensuring that every hour you spend training translates effectively into improved performance on the court.

Integrating these cross-training activities into your regular training schedule requires careful planning to avoid overtraining and ensure each activity complements your pickleball play. A well-rounded weekly training plan might include two days of strength training, focusing on different muscle groups each day; one day of flexibility work through yoga or Pilates; one day of agility drills with cones or an agility ladder; and one or two days of alternative cardiovascular training such as jogging or cycling. Ensure you schedule at least one rest day per week to allow your body to recover. This variety in training not only improves your overall fitness but also keeps your routine interesting and engaging, helping you stay committed to your fitness goals and enjoy your development as a pickleball player.

THE MENTAL GAME: PSYCHOLOGICAL TIPS FOR PICKLEBALL SUCCESS

Success in pickleball isn't solely a matter of physical skill and endurance; the mental aspects of the game play an equally critical role. Your ability to focus, manage pressure, and maintain mental toughness can often be deciding factors in both casual play and competitive matches. If you lose focus easily, you can easily underperform. Let's explore several techniques and strategies that can help fortify your mental game, ensuring you're as sharp mentally as you are physically when you step onto the court.

Focus Techniques

Maintaining focus during a pickleball game is crucial, especially in a sport where the pace can shift rapidly and distractions are frequent. Distractions could be external, like an intimidating opponent, someone yelling on the sidelines, or poor weather conditions. Or, distractions can be internal, like self-doubt, negative thoughts, and worrying about the outcome of the game. Both types of distractions will cause you to underperform if you don't learn to refocus.

Let's start with some techniques to help you focus during a game.

- **Refocusing Question:** When you find yourself getting distracted by something, ask yourself, "What's important now?" This will remind you that focusing on the distraction is unhelpful and will redirect your thoughts onto the task at hand.
- **Thought-Stopping Phrase:** This is a phrase that you repeat to yourself when you begin to experience unhelpful thoughts. The phrase should be short and easy to remember, like "Let it go; focus on the next play." Repeat the phrase in your mind when you feel your thoughts running out of control. This will help you to recenter and keep your mind focused on the game.

Once you have these techniques in place to refocus in the moment, you can begin to improve your overall focus. This way, distractions will have less of an impact on you. Both techniques require consistency to improve your focus over time.

- **Visualization Techniques:** Before a game, take a few minutes to close your eyes and visualize yourself playing. Imagine executing the perfect serve, returning difficult shots, and moving confidently across the court. This mental rehearsal can help

prepare your brain for the actual game, making you feel more prepared and less anxious.
- **Mindfulness:** Mindfulness involves being fully present in the moment, aware of your surroundings, and calmly acknowledging and accepting your thoughts and feelings. Set a timer for three to five minutes to start. Close your eyes and focus on taking deep breaths. When your mind wanders, gently redirect your focus back to your breathing. This trains your ability to keep your attention centered on the present moment (Straw 2023).

Handling Pressure

Pressure is an inherent part of any competitive sport, and pickleball is no exception. Learning to manage this pressure is essential for maintaining performance under stress. One simple yet effective technique is controlled breathing. When you find yourself feeling tense, focus on taking slow, deep breaths. Inhale deeply through your nose, hold for a few seconds, and then exhale slowly through your mouth. This process can help reduce physical symptoms of stress such as elevated heart rate and muscle tension, making it easier to stay calm and focused.

Positive self-talk is another powerful tool for managing stress on the court. Be mindful of the messages you're sending yourself during play. Replace critical or negative thoughts with affirmations or encouragements. Phrases like "I can make this shot," "I'm prepared for this," or "I'm here to have fun" can shift your mindset from anxiety and doubt to confidence and enjoyment. This shift can dramatically affect your ability to perform under pressure, turning nervous energy into a focused drive to succeed.

Mental Toughness

Mental toughness is about staying resilient in the face of challenges, whether it's a tough opponent, a bad call, or your own mistakes. Developing this toughness starts with accepting that setbacks are a part of playing pickleball. Instead of getting frustrated by mistakes, view them as opportunities to learn and improve. After a game, analyze your performance objectively instead of stewing over what went wrong: What did you do well? What can you do better next time? This reflective practice can help you turn experiences, good and bad, into fuel for personal growth.

Another aspect of mental toughness is persistence. On the court, this might mean staying focused and fighting for every point, even if you're behind. Off the court, it could mean consistently working on your skills, even when progress feels slow. Set small, achievable goals for each practice or match, and focus on meeting them, regardless of the game's outcome. This goal-oriented approach keeps your mind focused on growth and improvement, rather than on short-term setbacks.

Mental Game-Day Preparation

Preparing for a tournament or a critical game involves more than just practicing your strokes or warming up your muscles; it requires mental preparation as well. Try this game day ritual:

1. **Start your day with a mindfulness practice.** This will relax you and help you focus on the present moment.
2. **Set your goals for the game.** Instead of simply aiming to win, which can be dependent on many variables, set goals related to effort and execution, such as maintaining a positive attitude, using a specific shot effectively, or staying active on the court throughout the match.
3. **Set up a positive thought-stopping phrase to use during the match.** Telling yourself, "Let go and focus," or "I'm prepared for this" can recenter your focus away from negative self-talk and other distractions.

The key here is consistency. The familiarity of the ritual can provide comfort and build confidence, allowing you to start each game with a calm, focused, and positive mindset. These mental preparations not only prime you for optimal performance but also enhance your enjoyment of the game, reminding you why you play pickleball in the first place: for the love of the sport, the joy of improvement, and the thrill of competition.

INJURY PREVENTION AND MANAGEMENT IN PICKLEBALL

Pickleball, while not as high-impact as some racket sports, still carries its share of injury risks, particularly due to the quick starts, stops, and lateral movements inherent in the game.

Common Pickleball Injuries

- Ankle sprains occur when the ligaments that support the ankle stretch beyond their limits or tear during rapid changes in direction.
- Shoulder strains are also prevalent, often resulting from repetitive overhead motions such as serving or smashing the ball. Over time, overextending the shoulder and rotator cuff can cause damage and pain to the muscle.
- Pickleball elbow is a common injury to the elbow caused by inflammation of the tendons. It occurs due to repetitive motion in pickleball.
- Achilles tendonitis can occur due to repetitive stress on the tissue that connects the calf muscle to the heel bone. This normally begins as a mild ache, but ongoing tension can lead to tendon tears (Altru 2023).

Preventing Pickleball Injuries

- **Use proper equipment.** Make sure that your footwear is supportive with good traction to avoid unnecessary slips and falls. Supportive shoes will reduce your risk of foot, ankle, and leg injuries.
- **Stretch before playing.** A proper warmup and cooldown are necessary to reduce the risk of injury or muscle strain. Try out the routines listed earlier in this chapter.

- **Adopt proper playing techniques.** For instance, learning the correct footwork can not only improve your game but also minimize the risk of ankle injuries. This involves maintaining a balanced stance and using step-and-slide movements rather than large lunges, which can place excessive strain on your ankles. Similarly, mastering the proper technique for serves and volleys can help prevent shoulder strains. Ensure that you warm up adequately and use a paddle that is the appropriate weight and grip size to reduce stress on your shoulder.
- **Exercise regularly.** Regular strength training, focusing on the muscles around your core, ankles, and shoulders, can fortify these areas against the demands of sudden, intense movements during play.

Dealing with Pickleball Injuries

Even with preventive measures, injuries can still occur, and knowing how to handle them is key to a quick and safe recovery. The RICE method is a simple self-care technique to use as a first treatment for minor injuries, like a sprain. This method is most effective when applied immediately after the injury occurs and can significantly speed up the healing process (Gopal and Shepard 2024).

1. **Rest:** Rest the injured area to avoid further damage.
2. **Ice:** Apply an ice pack to reduce swelling and numb pain. Apply for 10 minutes, stop for 20 minutes, then repeat this cycle one or two times.

3. **Compression:** Wrap the injured area to prevent swelling. Use an elastic medical bandage. Wrap the injury so that it is snug but not tight. If the skin turns blue or feels numb or tingly, loosen the bandage.
4. **Elevation:** Raise the injured body part above the level of your heart. This will reduce pain, throbbing, and swelling.

However, not all injuries can be managed through self-care, and recognizing when to seek professional help is essential. The RICE method should not be used for fractured bones or dislocated joints. If you experience severe pain, swelling that worsens over time, or if the injured area is deformed or unable to bear weight, these could be signs of a more serious condition requiring a trip to the emergency room. Regular check-ups with a health professional can help you manage chronic issues and prevent them from worsening. These professionals can offer personalized advice and treatment options, including physical therapy, which can be crucial for recovery and preventing future injuries.

As you continue your pickleball journey, keeping these strategies in mind will enhance your performance and protect you from common injuries, ensuring that your experience with the sport remains positive and healthful.

Now, as we wrap up our exploration of physical and mental readiness in pickleball, remember that preparation extends beyond just mastering strokes or understanding the rules. Your body's physical condition, combined with mental resilience, plays a crucial role in not only how you perform but also how much you enjoy the game. From warming up properly to strengthening your body and mind, each aspect we've covered in this chapter forms an integral part of your overall readiness for pickleball. As we transition into the next chapter, we'll shift our focus to mastering basic techniques, where you'll learn to apply your physical and mental preparations to refine your skills and elevate your game.

MASTERING BASIC TECHNIQUES

Now that you understand the rules of pickleball and how to prepare for a game, it's time to play. We're about to cover all of the basic techniques of pickleball, from the serve, to the return hit, to the volley, to the dink, and more. These components are the fundamentals of a good game of pickleball. You need to master these basics before you move on to more advanced, strategic gameplay. Whether you're a complete beginner learning these moves for the first time or a seasoned player refining your skills, this chapter will benefit you.

THE ART OF THE SERVE: TECHNIQUES AND TIPS

Before we get into technique, let's go over a quick reminder of the serving rules.

1. A serve must always be made with an upward stroke. No hitting from above or the side.

2. The paddle must make contact with the ball below your waist.
3. The serve must land in the diagonally opposite service area.
4. At least one foot must be touching the surface behind the baseline.

Serve Types

In pickleball, understanding the different types of serves and when to use them can add depth to your game strategy.

- **Traditional Volley Serve:** This is the classic serve where you hit the ball before it hits the ground. This serve benefits from speed and power and is the most common pickleball serve.
- **Drop Serve:** The server may drop the ball from any height, from an open palm, and contact the ball after it bounces at least once. You cannot toss the ball or propel it downwards; you simply drop it. There are no restrictions on whether the ball must bounce within the court boundaries, as long as your feet are in the legal position. Because the ball will rarely bounce higher than mid-thigh height, you hit it from a lower contact point. You lose some power, but you can add extra spin to your serve. Drop serves are better suited to beginner players who want to make sure their serves are successful.
- **Power Serve:** The power serve, also known as the fast and low serve, is all about speed and depth. Struck firmly and low over the net, this serve skims just above the net at a high speed, making it difficult

for the opponent to react in time. To perform this serve, stand with an open stance while facing the net. Bend your knees slightly, then deliver a full swing while rotating your hips and core. The power in the shot should come from your full body. Aim to hit the ball relatively low over the net and as far back on the pickleball court as possible, near the baseline. The power serve is best used by a player who has control over where they place the ball, as it can easily fly out of bounds. Use this when you want to increase the pressure on a skilled opponent or when you need a quick point to regain momentum in the game.

- **Lob Serve:** The lob serve, also known as the high soft serve, is designed to arc high in the air, landing deep in the opponent's court, which forces them to hit their return from the baseline, potentially setting them up for a weak return. The mechanics of the lob serve are very similar to the power serve. The most important difference is the contact point. Your paddle should hit the pickleball on the underside of the ball, rather than at the back. Your follow-through should be aimed up at the sky rather than toward your opponent. You should still use your whole body to hit it, but your movement will likely be slower. This type of serve is great for beginners who need another serve to mix up gameplay (PrimeTime Pickleball n.d.-a).

Positioning and Posture

The effectiveness of your serve relies heavily on your positioning and posture. Proper stance and body alignment not only help in achieving more powerful and accurate serves but also prevent injuries. Stand with your feet shoulder-width apart, parallel to the baseline, with your weight evenly distributed. As you prepare to serve, shift your weight to your back foot to create a coiled effect; as you swing, transfer this weight forward, uncoiling and driving the power through your hips, torso, and finally, your arm. This sequential movement ensures an efficient transfer of energy, maximizing the power of your serve while maintaining control.

Remember to keep your grip loose on your paddle. Players tend to grip their paddle too tightly and choke off the power from transferring smoothly. A looser grip allows the power to flow from your legs, into your core, into your arm, and then through your paddle into the ball.

Practicing Consistency

Consistency in serving is key to becoming a reliable pickleball player. Regular practice helps refine your muscle memory, making accurate serves second nature. Set up targets on various parts of the court to practice different serve placements. For instance, place a cone near the baseline for power serves and one near the corners to practice your precision. Spend time during each practice session focusing solely on serving, aiming for at least 50 serves to various targets until your accuracy improves. Over time, this practice will help you feel more confident in your serving abilities. Once you have sufficient control over the ball and have conquered the power and lob serve, you can move on to a more advanced serving technique.

Advanced Serving Techniques

As you become more comfortable with basic serving techniques, experimenting with advanced methods can further enhance your game. Adding spin to your serves can make them unpredictable and difficult to return.

- **Short Angled Serve:** This is a placement serve intended to lead your opponent to the edge of the court. You aim to serve the ball just passed the non-volley zone and next to the sideline. This serve is ideal when it surprises your opponent and they have to run for the ball, so try not to make it too obvious that you're angling for the sideline. You need to have quite strong control over the ball as the target is small and you could easily land the ball in the non-volley zone or send it out of bounds.
- **Sidespin Serve:** This serve involves striking the ball with a sideways motion, creating lateral spin that makes the ball skid and stay low off the bounce. Make sure that you are still swinging in a low-to-high motion. Focus on "cutting" the ball from right to left as you hit it to generate a lot of spin. This is a very difficult shot to return and can easily throw your opponent off.
- **Topspin Serve:** This is a serve that comes off your paddle spinning forward end over end. For a topspin serve, snap your wrist upon contact to impart forward spin, causing the ball to dip quickly and bounce higher. Aggressive topspin will kick toward the opponent and be hard to read and time, making it very challenging to return. However, this is an

extremely challenging serve to master and will require a lot of practice. (PrimeTime Pickleball n.d.-a)

By mastering these serving techniques and incorporating them into your practice routines, you can significantly improve your effectiveness on the court. Serving is not just a means to start the point; it's an opportunity to take control of the game from the outset. With the right serve, you can dictate the pace of the play and put your opponents under pressure, making every serve count toward your success in pickleball.

MASTERING THE RETURN: STRATEGIES TO START STRONG

One of the most crucial moments in a game of pickleball is returning the serve. This is your first opportunity to take control of the rally and set the pace of the point. Effective return strategies not only neutralize your opponent's serve but can also shift them into a defensive position, giving you the upper hand.

1. **Anticipate the ball.** To start strong, developing your anticipation skills is key. By observing your opponent's body language and paddle positioning before they serve, you can predict where the ball might land. Notice if their body is squared up or angled, as this can give you clues about the direction of the serve. Also, watch their paddle's backswing and speed; a faster swing might indicate a power serve, while a slower, more controlled swing could

hint at a softer serve aimed for precision. When facing powerful and spin-heavy serves, positioning is crucial; stand slightly behind your baseline to give yourself more time to react. Keep your knees slightly bent and your paddle ready at chest height. This stance allows for quick movements and adjustments.
2. **Plant your feet.** Once you've anticipated the ball's trajectory, move into place, and plant your feet. Stopping puts you in a balanced position when you make contact with the ball, minimizing any unnecessary movements and ensuring greater accuracy and control. If your body is still in motion, it can be challenging to time your shot accurately.
3. **Pick your shot.** When the serve comes your way, having a strategy for where to place your return can make all the difference. Aiming for the corners of the court can force your opponent to run, disrupting their positioning and potentially leading to weaker returns from them. Alternatively, returning with depth—hitting the ball deep into your opponent's court—can prevent them from advancing to the net, keeping them on the back foot and opening the court for your next shot (Slowinski 2023).

Practical drills are essential for refining these return strategies. One effective drill involves marking target areas in the corners and deep center of your opponent's court. Practice hitting your returns to these areas. You can do this drill solo by serving to yourself and then returning, or with a partner who serves to you. Aim to hit a set number of successful returns to each target area during your practice sessions, which will help improve your accuracy and confidence in placing your returns during actual games.

THE VOLLEY: TIMING AND TECHNIQUE

To volley in pickleball is to hit the ball before it bounces. It is an essential move to master, no matter how you play pickleball. Mastering the volley can significantly elevate your game, allowing you to exert more pressure on your opponent and control the pace of play.

Here are some tips to help you perfect your volley:

- **Maintain an athletic stance.** Have your feet shoulder-width apart and facing forward, your knees bent, and your arms in a ready position. This stance will have you ready to move in any direction as you react to the incoming ball.
- **Position yourself at the non-volley line.** This is a defensive position from where you can return the ball without giving up space for your opponent to hit into. If you start retreating, you give your opponent the opportunity to land a soft shot in front of you.
- **Anticipate the ball.** This involves reading your opponent's body language and the speed and angle of the ball as it comes toward you. Good anticipation allows you to position yourself optimally, making it easier to hit a strong and accurate volley. To develop this skill, focus on your opponent's paddle when they hit the ball. Notice the speed, angle, and any spin they might apply. Over time, you'll start to predict the ball's path more

quickly and accurately, allowing you to react swiftly and with confidence.
- **Use a "hammer" grip.** Here, you hold the paddle as if it were a hammer so that the paddle is nearly vertical. The "V" of your hand, between the thumb and the index finger, should be on top of the paddle handle. This grip allows for a natural wrist position, offering stability and flexibility in shots. At a moment's notice, you can choose to dink volley with your forehand or backhand volley. Your paddle should always be out in front and up, ideally at chest level, which ensures that you are prepared to meet the ball quickly without having to make drastic movements that can throw off your balance.
- **Control your swing.** Don't aim to hit the ball with as much power as possible, because you'll only lose control in the process. Your arm should start extended and stay there during the entire motion. An easy way to stick to this is to make sure you can see your paddle during the entire play. Don't pull it back behind you to make the shot. The paddle will create enough lift and power with a short swing (Paddletek n.d.-a).

Practicing your volley skills is essential for improvement, and there are specific drills that can enhance your hand-eye coordination and reaction time. One effective drill is the "wall rally," where you hit volleys against a wall at varying heights and speeds. This drill helps you adjust your paddle angle and body position quickly, which is crucial during rapid volley exchanges in a game. Another useful drill involves volleying with a partner at close range, promoting quick reflexes and precise paddle control. Start slowly to ensure your accuracy, then gradually increase your speed as your confidence and skills improve.

However, even experienced players can make mistakes while volleying, and recognizing these common errors is key to improving your game.

- One typical mistake is swinging too hard, which can send the ball flying out of bounds or into the net. Instead, focus on meeting the ball with firm, controlled paddle contact. Keep in mind that the key to volleying correctly is controlling the power and precision of the shot.
- Another common error is poor footwork. Stepping into the non-volley zone, or kitchen, before hitting a volley is a fault. To avoid this, practice maintaining balance and controlling your movements so that your momentum does not carry you into the kitchen after a volley.

By understanding these common pitfalls and working on the fundamental techniques, you can turn your volley into a consistent and formidable part of your pickleball game. You can keep your opponents on their toes and dictate the pace of play from the net.

PERFECTING THE PICKLEBALL DINK: WHY AND HOW

A dink is a soft, delicately placed shot that just goes over the net into the opposing non-volley zone. This is similar to the drop shot, but the dink is hit from the non-volley line, whereas the drop shot is hit from the baseline.

Often regarded as a soft, calculated drop shot, the dink is much more than just a gentle tap over the net. It's a strategic maneuver designed to land in the non-volley zone so that your opponents can't volley the ball but must let it bounce before they hit it. Employing the dink effectively allows you to control the pace of the game, extending rallies and creating opportunities to outmaneuver your opponents by placing the ball just beyond their easy reach. You need to learn the right technique in order to hit a consistent, well-controlled dink.

1. **Maintain an athletic stance.** Have your feet shoulder-width apart and facing forward, your knees bent, and your arms in a ready position. This stance will have you ready to move in any direction as you react to the incoming ball.
2. **Prepare your paddle.** Hold the paddle with a relaxed grip and position it at a slight upward angle. This positioning helps impart a gentle arc to the ball, ensuring it clears the net but doesn't travel too high or too fast, making it difficult for your opponent to execute an aggressive return.
3. **Anticipate the ball's trajectory.** Too often, players mishit the ball because they do not watch it closely enough.
4. **Stay at the non-volley line.** You should be close to the net but outside of the kitchen to avoid faults. If you move back, you give your opponents more time to react to a shot.

5. **Hit under the ball.** When striking for a dink, get your paddle under the ball. Gently lift through your shoulder with a controlled motion.
6. **Control the height.** If you hit the ball from a compressed position, then you can engage your legs for stability and control. If you stand up, then your paddle will come with you and give the ball too much height, making it easily returnable. However, while you want to keep your dinks low and unattackable, make sure to give yourself enough room over the net (Townsend 2021).

To sharpen your dinking skills, incorporate specific practice routines into your sessions. One effective exercise is the cross-court dink drill, where you and a partner continuously dink the ball back and forth, aiming to keep it within the kitchen. This drill not only improves your accuracy but also helps you develop a softer touch.

Another beneficial practice routine involves dinking from different positions. Start at the center of the baseline, then move to one side and finally to the other, practicing your dinks from each position. This not only enhances your ability to hit accurate dinks from various angles but also prepares you for real-game scenarios where you might not be ideally positioned.

As you advance in your dinking strategy, exploring more complex techniques can add depth to your gameplay. Cross-court dinks are an advanced strategy that involves hitting the ball diagonally across the net into your opponent's kitchen. This shot can be particularly effective because it forces your opponent to cover more ground, potentially leading to errors or weaker returns. Additionally, practicing dinks from different positions on the court, including from the baseline or while moving laterally, can prepare you for any situation on the court. These advanced strategies not only improve your dinking ability but also enhance your overall game by making you a more versatile and unpredictable player.

Dinking is a technique that, when mastered, can profoundly impact your performance and success on the court. By understanding the purpose of the dink, perfecting the technique, and practicing consistently, you equip yourself with the skills to control the game's pace and outsmart your opponents. Whether you're engaging in a friendly match or competing in a tournament, a well-executed dink can be a game-changer, turning the tide in your favor and showcasing your tactical prowess in pickleball.

DEVELOPING A POWERFUL BACKHAND

Most pickleball players prefer their forehand to their backhand. This is because backhand shots can easily fly out of bounds. Improving your backhand in pickleball involves more than just swinging the paddle; it's about refining your technique to make each stroke powerful yet controlled. Let's dive into the fundamentals of this essential stroke, focusing on the grip, stance, and swing path, which are the building blocks for effective hitting.

1. **Maintain an athletic stance.** This serves as the foundation for a powerful and effective stroke. Your feet should be roughly shoulder-width apart, with knees slightly bent to keep you agile and ready to

move. The ideal stance is dynamic, balancing your weight slightly more on the toes than the heels, enabling quick, responsive movements.
2. **Use the hammer grip on your paddle.** A hammer grip is recommended as it can provide more power on backhand shots. This grip aids in providing a stable yet flexible hold, allowing for a natural wrist movement essential for adjusting the paddle's angle during different shots.
3. **Focus on your swing.** The swing path is critical in generating power and control in your strokes. Aim for a smooth and controlled swing, with additional focus on using your shoulder and back muscles to power through the ball, as the backhand typically requires more upper-body strength than the forehand. To enhance the power of your strokes while maintaining control, make sure to utilize the kinetic chain. This concept involves the transfer of energy from larger to smaller body parts. Start your stroke by rotating your hips toward the net as you begin your swing, followed by your torso, and finally, your arm and paddle. This sequential motion ensures that power generated from your lower body is transferred through your core, into your arm, and then in a powerful impact on the ball.
4. **Try both the two-handed and one-handed backhand.** The two-handed approach adds power and control and makes hitting topspin easier. A one-handed backhand is ideal for a ball hit toward your body, as it allows you to quickly defend yourself (The Dink Media Team 2023a).

Incorporating drills can significantly improve your backhand. One effective drill is the wall rally, you continuously hit the ball against a wall, this time alternating between forehand and backhand. This not only helps in building muscle memory but also enhances your ability to switch quickly between stroke types, a vital skill during fast-paced games. Another beneficial practice is to work with a coach or a ball machine. Set the machine to deliver balls to specific areas, challenging you to use forehand and backhand strokes under varied conditions, enhancing your adaptability and precision.

Analyzing and refining your stroke mechanics is crucial for ongoing improvement. Using video playback is an invaluable tool in this process. Record your practice or match play, then review the footage to observe your grip, stance, swing path, and body movement. Look for areas where your form breaks down or where inefficiencies appear. Coaches can provide invaluable feedback during this analysis, pointing out subtle nuances that you might not notice on your own. They can provide corrective techniques and drills to address specific issues, helping you fine-tune your strokes for maximum efficiency and effectiveness.

By focusing on these fundamental aspects and consistently practicing, you can develop powerful, reliable backhand strokes that will serve as crucial weapons in your pickleball gameplay. As you become more proficient in these strokes, you'll find that you can handle a wider variety of shots with greater confidence, pushing your opponents harder and making your play sessions more dynamic and enjoyable.

FOOTWORK FUNDAMENTALS: MOVING EFFICIENTLY ON THE COURT

In pickleball, as in life, every step counts. Footwork is your key to pickleball success. The way you move on the court can define your gameplay, making the difference between reaching a shot comfortably and missing it by a whisker. Too often, players lead with only their upper bodies. This just ends up with them becoming off balance. Proper footwork will ensure that you can:

- get to the ball in time;
- be in a balanced position to take your next shot; and
- engage your full body to transfer your energy into the ball.

Try out these techniques to improve your footwork on the court:

- **Anchor Foot:** In this technique, you'll keep one foot anchored to the ground while the rest of your body pivots around this foot. If the ball is hit to your right, you keep your left foot anchored and use the right to move forwards, sideways, or back. If the ball is hit to your left, you keep your right foot anchored and move only your left foot. This technique will maintain your balance as you move to hit the ball. It also helps you to easily get back into position for the next ball. Anchor foot is a great technique to use when you're playing at the non-volley line.
- **Split Step:** The split step is a great movement to quickly and efficiently change direction on the court.

This is a small hop you take as your opponent hits the ball, landing on the balls of both feet with your knees slightly bent. Landing on the balls of your feet readies you to move in any direction to quickly reach the ball. It's a proactive move that keeps you engaged, agile, and ready, rather than reactive. After the split step, depending on where the ball is headed, you'll transition into lateral movements or forward steps to reach the ball.

- **Lateral Movement:** Lateral movement, or side-stepping, is crucial in pickleball due to the wide yet short court. Practice moving side to side without crossing your feet, maintaining a low center of gravity. This technique will allow you to travel quickly across the court without crossing your legs and becoming unbalanced (Flamm 2024).

Remember, a key part of effective footwork is agility. To enhance your agility and speed, incorporate specific drills into your training sessions. Try one of the drills that we outlined in chapter two. Agility ladder drills are particularly effective as they improve foot speed, coordination, and spatial awareness—all critical for maneuvering around the pickleball court.

Footwork errors often occur when players find themselves out of position or when fatigue sets in, leading to lazy foot movements. Common errors include overreaching, where you stretch too far to one side without moving your feet, which can lead to a loss of balance and ineffective shots. To correct this, focus on taking quick, small steps instead of large lunges. Or, try out the anchor foot method, so that you don't overreach and unbalance yourself. Another frequent mistake is failing to pivot your feet when turning to reach a backhand or forehand from the baseline. This pivot is essential for aligning your body correctly with the shot, providing both power and accuracy. Practice the split step as your opponent hits the ball so that you're primed to pivot and turn in any way. Recognizing and correcting these errors in practice will lead to more fluid, efficient movement during games.

As you integrate these footwork fundamentals into your pickleball practice, you'll notice a marked improvement in how you move and position yourself on the court. Efficient movement not only enhances your ability to play but also reduces your risk of injury, keeping you in the game longer. With agility, speed, and the right positioning, you'll handle shots more effectively and challenge your opponents at every turn.

As we wrap up this discussion of footwork fundamentals, remember that each step on the court contributes to your overall game strategy. From the anchor foot to the split step to agile lateral movements, mastering these basic patterns sets the foundation for advanced play. Up next, we'll dive into advanced skills and strategies, building on the techniques you've learned to elevate your game further and prepare you for competitive play.

ADVANCED SKILLS AND STRATEGIES

As you continue to improve your pickleball ability, you'll want to start incorporating some different strategies into your gameplay. Many players, despite being regularly on the pickleball court, feel that they experience a plateau in their ability and improvements. Or, maybe you're just looking for some extra tips that will help you to *finally* beat that one person on the court... If you feel like it's time to take your gameplay to the next level, then try one of these advanced strategies.

Advanced skills in pickleball don't just enhance your ability to play; they transform how you think about and engage with every aspect of the game. In this chapter, we'll cover strategic serving, defensive and offensive plays, the art of shot selection, and advice to improve your doubles play.

STRATEGIC SERVING: WHERE AND WHY TO SERVE

Targeting Weaknesses

One of the most effective strategies in pickleball is to identify and exploit your opponent's weaknesses. Pay attention to their shot patterns and tendencies. Are they aggressive players who like to take risks? Or are they defensive players who like to play it safe? By understanding their style of play, you can adjust your game plan accordingly.

Most players, especially at the amateur level, will have a weaker backhand than forehand. Observing your opponent during warm-up and early gameplay can give you clues about which side is less reliable. Once identified, strategically aim your serves to challenge their backhand, increasing the likelihood of a weaker return. Similarly, if you notice a player favoring the backline, then you can choose to hit more balls to the non-volley zone, dragging them from their comfort zone. This isn't just about gaining a point but about applying constant pressure, forcing your opponent to play defensively. Over time, this can lead to frustration and fatigue, skewing the game in your favor.

Additionally, when you're playing competitively, you can choose to target the weaker player on the opposition. This means that you and your partner consistently hit the ball to the weaker or less experienced player to force that player to make a fault. While this can help you win points, it probably isn't the best thing to do in a casual game with friends or family (Strachan 2019).

If you find yourself on the receiving end of this targeted strategy, then you can try the "squeeze" pickleball strategy. Basically, this just means that you and your partner squeeze together on the court. Instead of covering 50% of the court each, the weaker player should only cover 25% of the court, and the stronger player shift over to cover 75%. Now, if the opposition wants to continue targeting the weaker player, they will have to be much more accurate with their shots. The stronger player is also able to get more aggressive with their shots. This will change the dynamic on the court, and the mounting pressure will cause the opposition to either fault or open the court again (Shields 2023).

Mixing Shot Types

Variety is not just the spice of life but also a key ingredient in a winning pickleball strategy. By mixing up your serve and shot types—from soft arcs that drop close to the net to powerful drives aimed deep into the court—you keep your opponent guessing and reactive rather than proactive. For instance, start with a soft serve that barely clears the net, drawing your opponent forward. Follow this with a deep, powerful serve that pushes them back. This variation can disrupt their rhythm and balance, making it difficult for them to settle into a consistent return strategy. Each serve type should be practiced until it can be executed with confidence under pressure. Remember, they could be observing you for patterns and weaknesses. Try not to do any hits that are too obvious and easy for the opponent to predict.

Where you place your serve can significantly impact the flow of the game. Serving with precision to specific zones on the court can force your opponent into uncomfortable positions, making it hard for them to return with strength or accuracy. Practice serving to both the left and right corners of the service box, as well as deep into the center. This practice not only enhances your accuracy but also your ability to control the game's pace. Placing your serves strategically within these areas can limit your opponent's return options and set you up for more aggressive play.

Balancing consistency with the occasional high-risk shot creates a dynamic that can keep your opponent guessing. Consistent shots build a rhythm and can lull the opponent into a false sense of security. Introducing a sudden, unexpected lob or a sharp angle shot can break this predictability, potentially leading to unforced errors from the other side of the net. The decision to implement a high-risk shot should be calculated, considering the current score, your confidence in the shot, and the match's overall tempo. This balance keeps your game flexible and responsive, allowing you to adapt to the unfolding dynamics on the court while continuously pressing your advantage.

Psychological Impact

The mental aspect of pickleball is often as challenging as the physical. Strategic serving can play a significant role in mentally pressuring your opponents. By consistently serving to their weaker side or mixing up your serves effectively, you create a psychological challenge. Opponents might begin to anticipate difficulty before the serve is made, leading to anxiety and errors. This mental pressure can cause them to lose focus and confidence, which might lead them to make more mistakes or lose morale, especially in a tight game.

These advanced serving strategies are techniques that, when mastered and applied judiciously, can turn the tide of any game in your favor. As you practice these methods, consider their impact not only on your play but on the overall dynamic of the match. By elevating your serving game, you set the stage not just to play but to outplay your opponents, making each serve a decisive, strategic act that moves you closer to victory.

DEFENSIVE PLAYS: KEEPING THE BALL IN YOUR COURT

In pickleball, as in many sports, a strong defense can be just as pivotal as a powerful offense. Your ability to defend effectively not only keeps you in the game during tough rallies but also sets the stage for turning defense into offense.

When we say defensive play, we're talking about focusing on neutralizing the opponent's attack, maintaining control of the point, and creating opportunities to switch to offense. Let's look at four strategies to make sure you're playing the best defense possible.

Master Your Positioning

The first step in building a solid defense is mastering positional defense. This concept revolves around your ability to cover the court efficiently and anticipate where the next shot will land.

One of the best strategies to achieve this is by guarding the middle line of the court. Most opponents will be aiming to hit the middle ground of the court. This is because the net is lower here, and they are less likely to hit the ball out of bounds. So, in a defensive play, your first goal should be the guard the middle line. In singles, make sure you stand ready in the middle. In doubles play, communicate with your partner before the game to decide whose responsibility the middle will be. Otherwise, you'll end up with the dreaded, "I thought you had it!" when the ball sails between the two of you.

Positioning yourself slightly behind the baseline in a ready stance with your paddle up and centered gives you the best chance to react to your opponent's shots. This stance allows for maximum mobility and prepares you to move in any direction, crucial for returning shots that are hit deep into your court or sharply angled. It's about finding the balance between being far enough back to handle deep shots and close enough to the net to respond to shorter plays. Regular drills that simulate actual game scenarios can help you find this balance, enhancing your ability to move quickly and efficiently around the court without sacrificing your readiness to hit a winning shot.

One effective way to improve your court coverage is by practicing your footwork, ensuring you can move quickly and smoothly in any direction. Developing quick footwork and court awareness can allow you to reposition after each shot, ensuring optimal coverage. Additionally, staying alert and keeping your eyes on your opponent's paddle can give you valuable clues about the direction and speed of the incoming ball, allowing you to position yourself optimally (Pickleball University 2022).

Avoid "No Man's Land"

In pickleball, no man's land is the mid-court area between the baseline and the non-volley zone. It's a difficult spot to defend because it's too far for a nice volley and too close for a good groundstroke. To avoid this area, commit to either the non-volley line or the baseline.

Mastering the use of the non-volley zone can significantly enhance your ability to neutralize aggressive opponents. The key is knowing when and how to move into and out of the kitchen. Typically, you should move into the kitchen to respond to soft shots that land close to the net, which are difficult to return powerfully if you're too far back. You should also use this position if your opponents are attacking with volleys. Once in the kitchen, your goal is to keep your returns low over the net, ideally aiming them just high enough to clear the net but low enough to make it difficult for your opponent to hit an aggressive shot in response.

Moving out of the kitchen is just as important, especially when dealing with opponents who prefer powerful baseline shots. If you're playing further back, commit to the baseline. This will give you the time to react to your opponent's shots and set up your return. From back here, you'll have more room to move around the court.

Transitioning quickly from the kitchen to the baseline requires agility and foresight. Be intentional in your transitions between these areas. Make no more than a shot or two as you move between each line, or you're simply exposing a weakness. If you are in no man's land, make sure that you're using the split step technique to stay light on your feet and anticipate the ball. Practice this transition by setting up drills that require you to move in and out of the kitchen, responding to a mix of soft and hard shots. This not only improves your physical ability to move but also helps you develop a sense of when such transitions are necessary, enhancing your overall defensive strategy (Pickleball University 2022).

Absorb Any Power Shots

Handling power shots, such as smashes, is another crucial defensive skill. These shots are challenging because of their speed and the limited time they give you to react. However, if you master the art of absorbing the power from your opponent's shots, you can return the ball safely and reset the point. This will typically happen when you are up at the non-volley line, and your opponent tries to blast a shot by you. Instead of being offensive with your return, you want to absorb the power of the ball and let it trickle back over the net.

To defend against power shots effectively, your paddle angle and body positioning are key. Hold your paddle in front of you, slightly angled toward the shot. Keep a light grip and a stable wrist. This position allows you to block the ball and direct it back into your opponent's court. Keep your knees bent and your body low, which helps maintain balance and readiness to move. Instead of swinging your paddle at the ball, absorb the shot's power by allowing your arms to give slightly upon impact, which can reduce the ball's speed and help you control your return. Then, give the ball a light push over the net. This is a great defensive shot, especially if your opponent likes to play at the backline.

These kinds of shots can slow down the pace of play, reset the court, and give you the opportunity to transition back into an offensive position. By absorbing power shots, you can use an unexpected dink, lob, or bounce to catch your opponent off-guard (Paddletek n.d.-b).

Turn Defense into Offense

Lastly, turning defensive plays into offensive opportunities is what separates good players from great ones. Defense is great, but winning pickleball is done by scoring more points than your opponent. This means looking for the right opportunities to take advantage of your opponent's poor play. Every defensive return presents a potential offensive setup if executed correctly.

For instance, a well-placed return from a powerful smash can set you up for a strategic shot if you place it in a difficult area for your opponent to reach, like the far corners of the court. Practice hitting your defensive returns with purpose, aiming for areas that are hard for your opponents to cover. This not only keeps you in the rally but also shifts the pressure back onto your opponent, creating opportunities for you to seize control of the game.

The ability to transition smoothly between offense and defense is a necessity for advanced pickleball. By being flexible between the two, you can dominate the court in any situation. In pickleball, the most successful players are those who can adapt their play in the moment (Luxe Pickleball 2024).

Once you master these defensive strategies—positional defense, avoiding no man's land, handling power shots, and transitioning defense into offense—you equip yourself with the tools to withstand and counteract the varied offensive tactics you'll encounter on the court. As you continue to practice and integrate these skills into your gameplay, you'll find that your ability to not just survive but thrive in defensive situations becomes a key component of your overall game strategy, allowing you to compete with confidence and resilience.

OFFENSIVE STRATEGIES: TAKING CONTROL OF THE GAME

Taking control of a pickleball game requires more than just reacting to your opponent's moves; it involves active strategizing and execution to dominate the play.

Offensive play involves aggressive strategies aimed at winning points through powerful drives, strategic placement, and net control. Here are five offensive strategies to help you win some extra points on the court.

Maintain Pressure

Maintaining offensive pressure is crucial in keeping your opponent on the defensive and controlling the pace and depth of the game. This continuous pressure can be achieved by varying the speed, spin, and depth of your shots, keeping your opponent guessing and reacting rather than planning their next move.

The easiest way to do this is by using your serve to gain an advantage. The serve is the one time when everything is under your control. Aiming your serve well, like by making the opponent return it from their weaker side, is a good way to control the play.

Deep drives are a great way to push your opponent back to the baseline, while sudden drops or soft dinks can draw them uncomfortably forward, disrupting their rhythm and balance. The key is to keep the shots varied and unpredictable, as a patterned play is easier to anticipate and counter. Mixing fast-paced volleys with sudden soft shots not only tests your opponent's physical agility but also their mental acuity, as they must constantly assess and reassess their strategy.

Use Feints

One effective way to take charge is by creating openings in your opponent's defense, which can be achieved through the use of feints and disguised shots. Feints involve making a movement that suggests you are going to play the ball in a particular manner or direction, only to change at the last moment. For instance, you might make a strong backswing as if to hit a power drive, only to soften your stroke at the last second, dropping a dink just over the net.

Disguised shots work on a similar principle but often involve more subtle changes in paddle angle or speed. You might approach the ball as if to volley it back swiftly, but instead gently lob it over your opponent's head. These tactics can wrong-foot your opponent, causing them to commit to a defensive position that leaves them vulnerable elsewhere on the court.

Position Yourself for Advantage

Utilizing the entire court plays a significant role in an effective offensive strategy. By stretching your opponent across the full width and depth of the court, you exploit their physical limits and create spaces for decisive shots. Achieving this involves not just power but precision and foresight.

Angled shots that pull your opponent wide off the court open up spaces for subsequent plays. Deep baseline shots followed by short dinks can keep your opponent running and stretch their ability to defend effectively. The objective is to make them cover as much ground as possible, inducing fatigue, which can lead to slower reactions and more mistakes. This tactic not only wears down their physical stamina but can also fray their focus, making it harder for them to mount a strong defense.

Force Errors

Forcing errors from your opponent is another effective way to dominate the game. A forced error occurs when you hit a shot that puts pressure on your opponent and causes them to make a mistake.

This can be done by introducing unexpected changes in the speed and spin of the ball. A sudden fast-paced drive after a series of slower plays can catch your opponent off guard, potentially leading to a missed or weak return. Similarly, incorporating spin variations, such as topspin or sidespin, can make the ball's trajectory and bounce unpredictable, complicating your opponent's return efforts. These variations force the opponent to constantly adjust their stance and paddle handling, increasing the likelihood of errors. The goal here is not just to win points but to subtly undermine your opponent's confidence and control over the game by turning their own reactions into vulnerabilities.

Use Topspin

Topspin is one of the best offenses in pickleball; it is a spin that makes the ball travel forward to your opponent, from 6 o'clock to 12 o'clock. These balls will get over the net but then swerve down toward the court. Topspin keeps the pickleball low and harder to return.

You'll need to manipulate the speed on your topspin volleys depending on how low the pickleball you're hitting is. The higher the pickleball, the more pace you can put on your volley. The lower the pickleball, the less pace you should put on it, or it will likely fly out of bounds.

This strategy can be used from the back court, the mid court, or from the non-volley line to put tremendous pressure on your opponent (PrimeTime Pickleball n.d.-b).

By mastering these offensive strategies, you position yourself not just to respond to the game but to redefine it, imposing your rhythm and style of play. This proactive approach doesn't just enhance your performance but also enriches your experience of the game. As you continue to develop and refine these tactics, you'll find that your ability to control and influence the game grows, leading to more rewarding and successful play. Through strategic offense, you can ensure you're in control of the game and in a good position to win the match.

MASTERING THE LOB AND SMASH

The Lob

A lob shot is a high-arching shot designed to go over your opponent's head and land deep in their court. It can be used either defensively, to reset a fast pace, or offensively, to score a point. This is a great strategy because it can catch your opponent off guard and force them to move quickly to the back of the court.

The key to a successful lob is not just in how you hit the ball, but also in recognizing the opportune moment to employ this tactic. Typically, the best time to use a lob is when your opponent is positioned near the net, aggressively waiting to volley or smash. By lobbing the ball over them, you force them to quickly backtrack, disrupting their stance and rhythm, often resulting in a less controlled return. The lob shot is most often used from the non-volley line, and it can be hit with topspin, backspin, or slice.

To execute a lob, your paddle grip and swing are pivotal. Use a hammer grip—this grip facilitates a smoother swing from low to high, essential for the lob's required trajectory. Start with your paddle below the ball and swing upwards in a fluid motion, aiming to hit the ball at a point that ensures it rises sharply but descends slowly. Aim for a nice high arc that will give the ball time to travel over your opponent's head. This technique requires practice, as the right touch will prevent the ball from going too high and giving your opponent too much time to react or too low, making it easy for them to smash. The best place to hit an offensive lob is the baseline, because it will force your opponent to move back quickly. Practicing with a partner who can simulate different net positions can greatly enhance your ability to judge and execute lobs under varied conditions.

The best way to land a successful lob is by hiding your intentions from your opponent. Ideally, you could stand in a dinking stance and then change to the lob shot last minute with a quick flip of the wrist. This will give you the element of surprise and increase your chances of success.

Defending against lobs is equally crucial, as a well-executed lob by your opponent can significantly shift the game's momentum. When you notice a lob coming your way, your immediate response should be to turn and run toward the baseline, keeping your paddle ready. The key is to judge the ball's trajectory quickly and decide whether you'll be taking it in the air or after a bounce. If the ball is within a comfortable reach, a volley return can be effective. However, if it's deeper, waiting for it to bounce and then returning with a controlled stroke often provides better placement and power, allowing you to regain your strategic position in the court. The best shot to return a lob is often the drop shot. This will force your opponent to move forward and give you more time to get back into position.

To hit the drop shot, aim for the non-volley line, and use a soft touch. However, if you choose to return the ball, make sure you get back into position at the baseline or non-volley line as soon as possible (Denahn n.d.).

The Smash

Now, let's delve into the smash, a powerful move that can decisively end a rally when executed with precision. The smash is an aggressive offensive shot, executed through a forceful hit, as high as the player can reach, and directed at a sharp downward angle.

The smash is ideally used when a ball is hit high enough and within your striking zone, allowing you to hit downward with significant force. The effectiveness of a smash depends greatly on your paddle grip, body posture, and the timing of your stroke. Stand in a neutral position facing your opponent, holding your paddle with a hammer grip. When you see the ball approaching above your head, pivot with one foot and step back with the other. Rotate your torso while drawing your paddle back, then drive it forward and downward, transferring your body weight through the ball. As you swing, make sure you use your shoulder, not just your elbow, to execute the shot. This motion not only generates power but also helps in directing the ball downward into your opponent's court. Make sure that you are aiming the ball to a gap in the court, either between your opponents or near a line (PrimeTime Pickleball n.d.-c).

Combining lobs and smashes within your game strategy can keep your opponent unbalanced and unsure, always guessing your next move. A well-placed lob can draw your opponent away from their preferred position, and an unexpected smash can capitalize on their momentary weakness. Regularly integrating these shots into your practice sessions will enhance your skill in switching seamlessly between them, reflecting a well-rounded, strategic approach to your pickleball gameplay. Effective use of lobs and smashes not only demonstrates technical prowess but also a deep understanding of strategic play, crucial for advancing in pickleball's competitive realms.

DOUBLES STRATEGY: WORKING EFFECTIVELY WITH YOUR PARTNER

In doubles pickleball, the synergy between you and your partner can be just as crucial as your individual skills. Effective communication and coordination can transform two good players into a formidable team. Here are four helpful tips to make sure that you can get the best out of your doubles play.

Communicate Clearly

It sounds obvious, but one of the foundational elements of achieving strong doubles coordination is the use of communication and signals. Get into the habit of calling "mine" or "yours" for each shot, especially if you're with an unfamiliar partner. Yell "out!" to warn your partner not to hit a ball that you're sure is flying out of bounds.

Since speaking loudly can tip off your opponents, many doubles teams use hand signals or subtle verbal cues to plan their next moves. These signals can indicate who will take the next shot, especially in situations where both players could potentially strike the ball, or suggest a strategic serve or return. For example, a simple hand behind the back with a number of fingers extended can indicate a desired serve placement, while a nod or a quick word might be used to decide who moves to handle a shot down the middle.

Make sure you bolster your team's confidence by complimenting your partner on a good play. Don't criticize your partner, it will just make them self-conscious and more likely to make mistakes.

Choose Your Positioning

Positioning and movement on the court are equally important. Both partners must cover the court efficiently without getting in each other's way.

Typically, one player takes a slightly forward position near the net, ready to volley, while the other covers the baseline, prepared to return deep shots. This arrangement, often referred to as "up-and-back" or "stacking," allows both players to utilize their strengths and cover more court. However, it's crucial that movements are synchronized; for instance, if one player moves to one side to cover a wide shot, the other must adjust accordingly to cover the open court.

However, it can be very beneficial for both players to be positioned at the non-volley line. After the serve, you can aim to quickly move toward the non-volley line to a position parallel with your partner. Remember, if you get caught in no-man's land, stop and use the split step so that you're ready to hit the ball. It may take two or three shots to get safely to the non-volley line.

Share Responsibilities

Sharing responsibilities is a strategic aspect that requires clear understanding and agreement. Teams often plan and practice these exchanges, deciding in advance who will handle certain types of shots based on their position and strengths. This division of responsibilities helps prevent confusion and collisions during play, ensuring that both players can contribute effectively without hesitation.

In pickleball doubles, it's common to designate one player to take all shots down the middle. This decision is usually based on who has the stronger forehand and backhand. Decide how far over the centerline the partner will take balls. Additionally, volley exchanges can be fast-paced and require quick reflexes. You and your partner should decide who will take lobs, most likely the faster partner even if the lob is on the other side of the court.

Adapt to Your Partner's Style

Adapting to your partner's style is perhaps one of the most nuanced aspects of doubles strategy. Every player has a unique style, pace, and preference in their gameplay. When partners take the time to understand and complement each other's strengths and weaknesses, the team becomes stronger than the sum of its parts.

For instance, if one player excels at aggressive, fast-paced play, the other might focus on consistency and setting up shots for their partner. Communicating openly about each player's comfort zones and strategizing around them can lead to more cohesive and strategic gameplay. Additionally, being supportive and adaptable, celebrating good shots, and encouraging each other after mistakes can significantly boost morale and team cohesion (USAP n.d.-b).

Through these strategies—effective communication, planned positioning, shared responsibilities, and adapting to each other's play styles—you and your partner can enhance your coordination and play more effectively as a team. The key lies in mutual understanding, respect for each other's abilities, and a shared commitment to good play. As you continue to develop your partnerwork, you'll not only improve your performance but also your enjoyment of the game, making each match a rewarding experience of teamwork and skill.

A great team is made not just from individual skill but from how well partners work together. The strategies discussed here aim to create a deeper connection and coordination between partners, ensuring unified gameplay. Looking ahead, the next chapter will delve into overcoming common challenges in pickleball, equipping you with the knowledge to handle and adapt to various playing conditions and scenarios, ensuring that you're prepared no matter what the game throws your way.

SHOW OTHERS WHAT A DILL-LIGHT THE SPORT OF PICKLEBALL IS!

Paddles up, stress down.

— ANONYMOUS

In Chapter One, I mentioned how pickleball was born of the need for a sport that could unite people, regardless of their age, physical ability, or expertise in racket sports. Of course, almost from the start, pickleball stopped being simply an activity to kill boredom and began appealing to those into competitive play. The USA Pickleball Association has played a vital role in promoting the growth of the sport, and social media has helped expand its reach globally. However, those who haven't seen a game online or in person may confuse pickleball with other more challenging pursuits like paddle tennis or even tennis.

If you have already started playing your first games, then you have probably noticed the extent to which pickleball differs from these games. It is affordable, adaptable to all levels, and incredibly accessible and inclusive. Despite being easy to learn, however, it offers a depth and complexity that keeps players on their toes as they work to improve their skills.

Those who play pickleball regularly know that it is easy to forget you're even exercising when you're enjoying a game. Yet the sport has so many benefits, including better cardiovascular health, coordination, and agility. If you're already noticing the changes this sport is bringing to your physical and mental health, I hope you can share your discoveries with others.

By leaving a review of this book on Amazon, you'll show others where they can find a complete guide to playing pickleball with a winning strategy.

Those who already play pickleball, meanwhile will also benefit, as the book contains many advanced techniques that can help them overcome their toughest challenges.

Thanks for your support. Many more powerful tips lie ahead, so enjoy the rest of your reading experience!

Scan the QR code below

OVERCOMING COMMON CHALLENGES

From beginners to advanced players, everyone is going to experience some sort of challenge on the pickleball court. In this chapter, we'll provide simple and comprehensive guides to dealing with all of the common challenges in pickleball. This chapter includes navigating the non-volley zone, handling high-pressure situations, overcoming ability plateaus, dealing with different weather conditions, recovering from equipment malfunctions, and clarifying common rule misunderstandings.

NAVIGATING THE NON-VOLLEY ZONE: TECHNIQUES AND TACTICS

The non-volley zone, or the kitchen, is a strip that extends seven feet on either side of the net and is one of the most distinctive features of a pickleball court. It is also one of the things that most new players get confused about. This zone is crucial because no volleying is allowed within it; you must let the ball bounce once before hitting it if you are standing in this area. Let's clarify what you can and cannot do in the non-volley zone.

- You cannot step on the non-volley line or into the non-valley zone while (a) actually hitting a volley, (b) during your follow-through, or (c) as a result of your momentum.
- No part of your equipment can touch the non-volley zone during a volley. Even if your hat falls off and lands in this zone as you volley, that counts as a fault!
- You can enter the non-volley zone at any time, but it doesn't make much strategic sense to stand there. It's better to stand just behind the non-volley line so that you can move into the kitchen or back on the court when necessary.
- You can hit a ball inside the non-volley zone only after it has bounced.
- A serve cannot land in the non-volley zone (IntoPickleball n.d.).

Now, let's look at some tips to make sure you're navigating the non-volley zone correctly:

- **Be aware of your positioning.** Always be conscious of where you are on the court in relation to these lines. During play, as you move forward toward the net, it's vital to stop just behind the kitchen line to volley, ensuring you do not step into the zone unless the ball bounces first. Practicing this spatial awareness can be as simple as doing drills that involve moving in and out of the kitchen, helping

you get a physical sense of the space and how to manage your movements in relation to the zone.
- **Move strategically.** Often, it can be really beneficial to stand at the non-volley line. However, make sure you're positioning yourself in a way that maximizes your ability to control the play. When it's advantageous, stepping into the kitchen to take a shot after the bounce can be a strategic move. Another good strategy is to back up during fast exchanges, as the extra distance can give you some more time to react. If you notice the game speeding up, you can take a quick hop back from the non-volley line and into the split step to be ready for the next shot.
- **Pick your shot.** The dink is the most common and strategic shot used from the non-volley line. Executing a successful dink involves hitting the ball just high enough over the net to clear it, but soft enough so that it lands softly in the opponent's kitchen, making it difficult for them to return with force. You can vary this shot with a lob or smash to go deeper into the court and catch your opponent off guard (Shields 2022).

In mastering the non-volley zone, you not only enhance your defensive and offensive game but also deepen your strategic understanding of pickleball. The kitchen can be a complex area to navigate, but with practice, you'll soon be able to manage it with ease. By focusing on the techniques and strategies highlighted, you're better prepared to face and overcome the challenges this unique area presents, turning potential obstacles into opportunities for game-winning plays.

HANDLING HIGH-PRESSURE SITUATIONS IN MATCH PLAY

Another common mistake I see in pickleball is players buckling under pressure. When the score tightens and every point starts to feel like it could tip the scales, the pressure on the pickleball court can become palpable. It's far too easy to become overwhelmed and start making silly mistakes. When we lose focus, we can forget everything we've remembered in training. Whether it's a crucial match point or a tense tiebreaker, your ability to maintain composure and focus under pressure is what can set you apart from competitors. Let's explore some effective techniques and strategies to navigate these stressful moments, ensuring that you can play your best game possible.

- **Focus on what you can control.** Instead of focusing solely on winning the match, set goals related to your performance, such as maintaining a positive attitude, communicating effectively with your doubles partner, or applying a specific strategy you've been practicing. This shift in focus helps alleviate the pressure of the score outcome and places your attention on elements you can control, keeping you grounded and focused in the match.
- **Visualize your performance.** Visualization is a powerful tool in your mental preparation arsenal. Take time before matches to close your eyes and imagine yourself successfully navigating tough

scenarios. See yourself serving accurately, returning challenging shots, and moving confidently around the court. This mental rehearsal primes your brain to perform these actions in real life, reducing anxiety and boosting your confidence when those critical moments arise.
- **Take some deep breaths.** Breathing exercises are invaluable for managing stress and maintaining concentration before intense match play. A simple yet effective technique is deep, diaphragmatic breathing. By focusing on taking slow, deep breaths, you engage the parasympathetic nervous system, which helps counter the body's stress response. Practice this technique regularly, not just before matches, so it becomes a natural part of your response to stress. Before a game, or between sets, if you feel the pressure mounting, take a moment to close your eyes and focus on your breathing—inhale deeply through your nose, hold for a few seconds, and exhale slowly through your mouth. This can significantly calm your nerves and refocus your mind on the game.
- **Understand that stress can benefit you.** As you head into a big game, you will more than likely feel stressed. However, you can decide if this stress works for you or against you. Learn to accept the presence of stress, and tell yourself that it means you are excited. This will energize you and give you the needed adrenaline to win the game. Don't let your stress consume you, or turn into anxiety.
- **Practice decision-making under pressure.** When the game speeds up, there's a natural tendency to

speed up your reactions. However, this can lead to mistakes or poor shot choices. Practice making deliberate decisions in practice games or drills. Set up scenarios where you must make quick decisions and focus on the process of making these decisions calmly and accurately. Over time, this practice will help improve your ability to remain thoughtful and deliberate in your shot selection, even when under pressure. You can incorporate decision-making drills into your practice sessions. For example, have a coach or fellow player shout out different game situations ("down by two points," "match point," etc.) and practice what shot or strategy you would deploy. This not only improves your quick thinking but also prepares you for similar stressors during actual matches.
- **Learn from your experience.** Finally, use high-pressure situations as learning opportunities. Reflect on these experiences to understand what worked, what didn't, and how you can improve. You can keep a journal to log your thoughts. After each match, especially those that involve high-pressure moments, take some time to jot down key takeaways. What strategies helped you remain calm? What mistakes did you make under pressure? How did you feel physically and mentally during crucial points? Reflecting on these questions can provide valuable insights that you can apply in future games (Asics 2021).

Handling pressure effectively in pickleball involves a combination of mental preparation, physical readiness, and reflective practice. By integrating these strategies into your routine, you'll not only enhance your ability to perform under pressure but also enrich your overall experience and enjoyment of the sport. Remember, each high-pressure situation is a step toward becoming a more seasoned and skilled player, equipped to handle whatever the game throws your way.

OVERCOMING PLATEAUS: TIPS FOR CONTINUED IMPROVEMENT

I recently had a friend reach out to me, seeking advice. They explained that when they began playing pickleball, they felt that they were improving every day. However, now that they are a year into playing, they feel like their improvements have hit a plateau. They're frustrated and irritated that they can't seem to get any better. Unfortunately, this is a common experience is many sports. Progress isn't always a steady climb; there are moments when improvements seem to stagnate and scores plateau. The question is, how can you overcome a plateau?

Understand the Process

The first thing to understand is that hitting plateaus is completely normal! Many athletes will make huge strides in their performance early on in their training. As you get better, your improvements will slow down and maybe halt.

Recognizing these plateaus is the first step toward overcoming them. You might notice that despite regular practice, your skill level or game scores aren't improving. Perhaps you find yourself making the same mistakes repeatedly, or your usual strategies no longer seem effective against your regular opponents. This stagnation can be frustrating, but it's a common part of learning and improving in any skill.

Adopt a Growth Mindset

When you identify a plateau in your ability, you have the choice to quit, settle at your current level, or put in the effort to become great. Instead of complaining that you're working hard and not getting any better, choose to dig deeper. Stay disciplined and see this as an opportunity to refine and expand your skills.

Setting new goals is a fundamental strategy in this process. These goals should push you slightly out of your comfort zone but remain achievable. For instance, if you find your serve has stopped improving, set a goal to master a new type of serve like the spin serve or the drop serve. Incorporate specific, measurable targets such as, "I will practice my new serve for 30 minutes each day," or "I will use the spin serve in at least three game situations each match." This approach not only renews your focus but also diversifies your skills, keeping your practice sessions dynamic and engaging.

Cross-training is another effective method to push past a plateau. Engaging in activities outside of pickleball can enhance your physical fitness, which in turn, can improve your game. For example, participating in sports like tennis or badminton can improve your hand-eye coordination and agility, while activities like yoga or Pilates can enhance your flexibility and core strength, all of which are beneficial for pickleball. Additionally, mental exercises, such as chess or puzzle-solving, can sharpen your strategic thinking, helping you to see your pickleball game from new perspectives and develop innovative strategies on the court.

Use Your Available Resources

Seeking and utilizing feedback is essential in overcoming plateaus. Ideally, regular input from coaches can provide you with insights into areas of your game that need improvement, which might not be evident to you. If this is too costly for you, then peer feedback can offer perspectives on changes in your gameplay over time, which can help you track your progress more accurately. Moreover, engaging in self-analysis is crucial; take time after games to reflect on your performance. Identify specific instances where a different approach or strategy might have yielded a better outcome and think about how you can incorporate these changes into your practice sessions.

Don't limit your learning to the people around you. Use YouTube to learn drills, techniques, and activities to help you improve your game. Make sure you're watching professional games so that you can observe the best pickleball athletes. These players are the best for a reason. What can you learn by watching how they play (West 2016)?

By embracing these strategies, you not only overcome plateaus but also enrich your overall experience and enjoyment of pickleball. Each challenge you encounter and navigate adds depth to your understanding of the game and enhances your skills in ways that steady, unchallenged play never could. Therefore, view each plateau not just as a hurdle but as an invitation to deepen your mastery of pickleball and discover new joys in this engaging sport.

DEALING WITH ADVERSE WEATHER CONDITIONS

Many people play pickleball outdoors, which exposes you to a variety of weather conditions, each bringing its own set of challenges. Understanding how to adapt your gameplay to these conditions can significantly enhance your performance and enjoyment of the game. Whether it's the gusty winds that challenge your shot accuracy, the scorching heat that tests your endurance, or the biting cold that affects your grip and ball control, each condition requires a thoughtful approach.

Playing in Wind

Wind can be one of the most challenging weather conditions in pickleball, as it unpredictably affects the ball's trajectory. Here are some tips to help you adapt your game for windy conditions.

- **Adjust your shot selection.** When playing in windy conditions, it's crucial to adjust your shots. First, consider using lower, faster shots, such as drives, rather than high lobs or soft dinks that the wind could easily catch and divert. This strategy reduces the wind's impact on your play. Additionally, adjust your serve to be less aggressive and more focused on placement rather than power to ensure it lands within bounds despite gusty conditions. You can also

use more topspin to counteract the effects of the wind.
- **Choose the right side.** Positioning is also key. If possible, choose the side of the court where the wind is at your back. This will give your shots more power and control. If you're playing into the wind, stand further back than usual to compensate for the wind slowing down the ball.
- **Be patient.** If you're serving, you can wait a moment for a strong gust of wind to blow over. Wait for the right opportunity to hit any aggressive shots, because the wind will make it difficult to control the ball.
- **Use the wind to your advantage.** Another effective strategy is to use the wind to your advantage by hitting shots where the wind will throw your opponents off. For instance, if the wind is blowing from side to side, you can serve or return shots aiming just inside the sideline. The wind can push the ball further to the side, making it more difficult for your opponent to return. Observing and adapting to how the wind affects the ball during the warm-up can give you valuable insights into how to adjust your play. This proactive approach not only mitigates the challenges posed by the wind but also turns the weather into a strategic ally.

Playing in Heat

Sunshine is the best weather for playing pickleball. However, when the heat becomes extreme, things can get pretty uncomfortable. For one, the brightness can affect your visibility. However, the biggest challenge is physical exertion and dehydration. Managing your body's response to heat is crucial to maintaining performance and preventing heat-related illnesses.

- **Stay hydrated.** Hydration is your first line of defense. Ensure you drink plenty of fluids before, during, and after play. It's advisable to hydrate with beverages that replace electrolytes lost through sweat, alongside regular water intake.
- **Wear a hat and sunglasses.** These will reduce the glare from the sun, protect your face, and improve your visibility on the court.
- **Apply sunscreen.** Even on cloudy days, the UV rays can be really strong. Make sure you're applying sunscreen regularly so that you don't get burnt.
- **Wear light-colored, breathable clothing.** This can significantly help manage heat by reflecting rather than absorbing sunlight and allowing better air circulation.
- **Use cooling towels.** A damp cloth can be draped around your neck during breaks to help lower your body temperature.
- **Adjust your play times.** If possible, schedule your games during cooler parts of the day—early morning or late evening. If you must play during peak heat, take regular breaks to rest in the shade and hydrate. Shortening the games or playing fewer games can also reduce the risk of heat exhaustion. Always listen to your body—dizziness, headache, and nausea are signs that you need to stop and cool down.

Playing in Cold Weather

Cold weather affects how you handle your equipment and how the pickleball behaves.

- **Adjust your warm-up routine.** In colder weather, you need to spend more time warming up to prevent any injuries.
- **Hit with more force.** In colder temperatures, pickleballs become harder and less responsive, requiring you to hit with more force while maintaining control.
- **Wear the right clothing.** Layering is key; it allows you to adjust your body temperature as you warm up or as conditions change. Thermal compression garments can keep your muscles warm and flexible, reducing the risk of injury. Gloves designed for racket sports can improve grip on the paddle when your hands are cold.
- **Choose the right ball.** Some balls are designed to perform better in lower temperatures. These balls are usually softer, helping compensate for the hardening effect the cold has on standard balls. Experiment with different balls during your warm-up to find one that performs best in the conditions of the day (11 Six 24 Pickleball 2023).

Adapting Game Strategy

Flexibility in your game strategy is crucial when playing in variable weather conditions. This means being ready to modify your usual style of play based on the current conditions. For instance, windy conditions might necessitate a more conservative game focused on placement rather than power. Hot weather might mean conserving energy by playing a more strategic, less aggressive game. Cold conditions might require a more forceful playstyle to compensate for the reduced bounce and responsiveness of the ball.

Incorporating these adaptations into your game plan can significantly enhance your ability to perform under diverse conditions. By continuously assessing the environment and adjusting your strategies accordingly, you maintain a level of play that can challenge your opponents and bring out the best in your game, regardless of the weather.

EQUIPMENT MALFUNCTIONS AND ON-THE-FLY FIXES

Like any frequently used gear, your pickleball equipment is prone to wear and tear or sudden malfunctions that can impact your game. Understanding common equipment issues and knowing how to address them quickly can keep you in play and prevent these minor setbacks from ruining your match-day experience. Here are some common equipment issues in pickleball:

- **Paddle Wear:** One of the most frequent issues you might encounter is paddle wear. Over time, the surface of your paddle can become smooth, losing its texture and grip on the ball, which will affect your control and power.
- **Grip Loosening:** Another common issue is the loosening of the paddle grip. This usually happens

due to the grip tape wearing out or the adhesive weakening, which can lead to a less secure hold on your paddle, affecting your swing accuracy and comfort.

- **Ball Degradation:** Ball degradation is also typical, especially for those frequently playing outdoors. Exposure to elements like sunlight and moisture can harden the ball or alter its texture, impacting its bounce and flight characteristics.

So, what do you do when faced with these issues? Knowing some quick, temporary fixes can be incredibly handy. For a loosening grip, a simple solution is to carry a roll of athletic or grip tape in your bag. If you notice the grip becoming loose mid-game, a quick re-wrap with tape can secure your handle and improve your control until you can perform a more permanent replacement. For minor paddle surface wear, sometimes wiping the surface with a slightly damp cloth can remove dust and restore a bit of its original texture, offering a temporary fix until you can further assess the wear post-match.

To avoid any malfunctions during a game, do a quick pre-match check of your gear. Before each game, take a moment to inspect your paddle for any signs of wear or damage. Check the grip to ensure it's secure and comfortable, and give your paddle a few test swings to make sure everything feels right. Inspect your pickleballs too; look for cracks or significant wear that could affect their performance. This pre-game inspection helps identify potential issues before they affect your play, ensuring you step onto the court with equipment that's up to the task.

Obviously, if you notice that your pickleball equipment is seriously deteriorating, you need to replace it. You may need to replace your paddle grip every few months, depending on how frequently you play. Otherwise, replace it whenever it begins to feel worn or uncomfortable. For the paddle surface, regular cleaning and avoiding harsh impacts or surfaces that can cause scratches or dents are good practices. Store your paddle in a cool, dry place out of direct sunlight to help prevent material degradation. As for pickleballs, rotating your stock and using different balls for practice and competitive play can help maintain their quality. Also, investing in higher-quality balls can be more cost-effective in the long run as they tend to withstand wear better and offer consistent play.

By maintaining a regular check and care routine for your pickleball equipment, you not only ensure optimal performance but also save on potential costs from premature replacements. Knowing how to handle on-the-fly fixes keeps you prepared for unexpected issues, ensuring they don't derail your enjoyment or success in the game. Always remember, the better you care for your equipment, the better it will perform when you need it most, letting you focus fully on your game and the enjoyment of pickleball.

COMMON RULE MISUNDERSTANDINGS AND HOW TO CLARIFY THEM

In the realm of pickleball, as in any sport, understanding the rules is fundamental to playing the game correctly and enjoying it to the fullest. However, certain rules in pickleball can be particularly perplexing, leading to common misunderstandings that might affect your gameplay. Here are a few areas where players normally misunderstand the rules:

- **The Double Bounce Rule:** One rule that often trips up new players is the double bounce rule. If you've played a lot of tennis, you will probably instinctively rush forward after the serve to try and hit the ball. But in pickleball, the double bounce rule requires that the ball must bounce once on each side of the net before volleys are allowed. The purpose is to slow the game down slightly, giving the receiving team a fair chance to respond after the serve. Misunderstanding this rule can lead to faults that might cost you points. To internalize this rule, practice drills that emphasize letting the ball bounce once on each side before initiating a volley. This not only cements the rule in your gameplay but also sharpens your reaction time and strategic planning about when and where to volley.
- **Service Sequence:** Another rule that often causes confusion is the service sequence, especially in doubles play. In pickleball, the server must call out three numbers before each serve: the serving team's score, the receiving team's score, and, in doubles, which server they are—either the first or second. This sequence dictates the server's position and helps keep track of the serving order, which can get particularly tricky in doubles. Miscommunication or forgetting to call the score can lead to faults or even arguments on the court. To avoid these issues, make a habit of verbally reviewing the score and server sequence with your partner before each serve during

practice games. This not only helps you internalize the sequence but also ensures clear communication with your partner.

- **The Role of Officials:** The role of officials in tournaments is another area where clarity is important. Officials are responsible for ensuring that the rules of pickleball are upheld during matches. They make calls on faults, keep track of the score, and ensure that the game runs smoothly. Knowing how to interact effectively with officials can greatly enhance your tournament experience. Always address officials respectfully and ask for clarifications calmly if you're unsure about a call. Remember, officials are there to help maintain the integrity of the game—understanding their role and respecting their decisions are key to a fair and enjoyable match.

- **The Hindrance Rule:** While this is not yet a pickleball law, it is likely to be incorporated into the USAP rulebook by 2025. This rule dictates that singles should not talk during points and that doubles players should not talk when the ball is moving toward their opponent's court. This is because any talking can interfere with an opponent's ability to hit the ball, known as a hindrance. For example, if you hit a lob and yell at your opponent to "get back!" distracting them and causing them to miss the ball, then they may claim the point based on deliberate hindrance (USAP 2024).

For players keen on deepening their understanding of pickleball rules, several educational resources are available. The official rulebook published by the USA Pickleball Association (USAP) is a comprehensive resource that details every rule and regulation of the game. This rulebook is available both online and in print, providing easy access for players seeking to clarify or refresh their understanding of the rules. Additionally, online forums and pickleball websites offer a platform for discussion and advice, where you can pose questions and share experiences with other players. Participating in certified coaching sessions can also be helpful. These sessions not only focus on improving your physical game but also emphasize rule comprehension, ensuring that you're well-versed in the nuances of the game.

Make sure that you're promoting rule awareness among your peers to enhance the playing experience for everyone. Encouraging open discussions about confusing rules can help prevent misunderstandings during play and foster a more knowledgeable and respectful pickleball community. Don't play by looser or modified rules in practice games, as you will probably repeat one of these habits in a match.

By focusing on these aspects, you not only enhance your own understanding and enjoyment of pickleball but also contribute to a broader appreciation and adherence to the rules within your playing circle. This not only makes the game fairer and more enjoyable for everyone but also upholds the spirit of respect and sportsmanship that is central to pickleball.

As we close this chapter on overcoming common challenges in pickleball, remember that each obstacle you encounter on the court is an opportunity for growth. Whether it's mastering complex rules, adapting to adverse weather conditions, or overcoming a plateau, each challenge allows you to deepen your understanding and enhance your skills, making you a more competent and confident player. As you move forward, carry these lessons with you, ready to tackle whatever the game throws your way in the next match. Keep this spirit of learning alive as we transition to the next chapter, where we'll explore the joys and benefits of pickleball, not just as a sport, but as a means to enrich your life and foster community connections.

PRACTICE MAKES PERFECT

So, you know the rules of the game, you know the best times to dink or lob or smash the ball, and you know the mechanics of how to execute these shots. Now what? Now, you practice. This is the most important thing you can do to improve your pickleball. In this chapter, we'll provide some fun drills guaranteed to hone your pickleball skills, either by yourself, with a partner, or as a team. Next, we talk about how you can use technology to take your practice to the next level. To finish, we discuss how to create a personal practice schedule and measure your improvements over time. Let's begin!

SOLO DRILLS FOR SKILL ENHANCEMENT

Stroke Practice Against a Wall

An important pickleball skill is your ability to consistently execute strong and accurate forehand and backhand strokes.

One of the most effective ways to enhance these skills is by practicing against a wall, a fence, or a rebounder. This drill allows you to receive immediate feedback on every stroke you make, helping you adjust your swing, angle, and power in real time. Start by focusing on your forehand; hit the ball against the wall, aiming to keep the ball within an imaginary box. You can even put some tape on the wall at pickleball net height (34 inches) and aim to keep hitting above that line. The goal is to maintain a rhythm where you can control the ball's pace and direction with each hit. After several sessions, switch to your backhand and apply the same principles. This method is cheap, easy, and convenient.

Serve Precision

Your serve sets the tone for each point in pickleball. Many players consider this the most important skill in the sport. Stand at one side of the court and practice hitting the ball into the opposite service box. This repetitive practice will help you increase your accuracy and confidence. If you want to challenge yourself, set up targets in different zones of the court to practice serving accuracy and power. Use cones or markers to designate target areas where you typically want your serves to land. Practice hitting these targets consistently, varying your serve speed and spin to simulate different match scenarios. This drill enhances your ability to start the game on your terms, placing the ball precisely where your opponent least expects it. Over time, this precision in serving can significantly improve your ability to control the game right from the serve.

Footwork Ladders

As we discussed in earlier chapters, agility ladders are an excellent tool for improving footwork speed and precision, which are crucial for effective movement on the pickleball court. Lay out an agility ladder on a flat surface and perform various footwork drills such as the two-foot hop, the lateral shuffle, or the in-and-out drill. Each of these movements trains different aspects of footwork agility that are critical during gameplay. For example, the two-foot hop improves your ability to maintain balance and readiness after moving, while the lateral shuffle enhances your side-to-side movement speed, crucial for reaching those wide shots. Regular ladder drills can significantly increase your footwork efficiency, making you quicker and more agile on the court.

Shadow Playing

If you have no equipment at home, it's still possible to practice. Shadow playing involves practicing your pickleball strokes and movements without a ball. This method allows you to work on your form by focusing entirely on your body mechanics and stroke technique. Visualize different game scenarios, such as returning a serve or approaching the net for a volley. As you shadow play, pay attention to your foot placement, paddle positioning, and body posture. This drill is particularly useful for correcting form and improving your physical response times. By repeatedly practicing your strokes and movements, you solidify your muscle memory, enhancing your overall gameplay without the distraction of a ball. Tennis players have been using this technique for years (Racket Royalty 2023).

By integrating these solo drills into your regular practice sessions, you are sure to see improvements in your precision, power, and agility. As you progress, these drills will not only improve your physical skills but also boost your confidence, preparing you for any challenge that comes your way on the court. Remember, the path to perfection in pickleball is a continuous journey, and every practice session is a step toward mastering the art of the game.

PARTNER DRILLS TO ENHANCE COORDINATION AND REFLEXES

Partner drills are another great way to improve your skills. These drills are designed to simulate real game scenarios, providing both players with great experience. These exercises not only fine-tune your individual skills but also enhance your coordination and reflexes as a team, which are crucial during competitive play. Let's explore some specific partner drills that focus on cross-court rallies, volley-to-volley exchanges, cooperative dinking, and power shot exchanges, each designed to elevate your game through collaborative practice.

Cross-Court Rallies

Engaging in cross-court rallies with a partner is an excellent way to develop your directional control and anticipation skills.

- Stand diagonally across from your partner at opposite ends of the court.

- Consistently hit the ball to each other, aiming for it to cross the court each time.

This not only helps in practicing your aim but also in predicting where the ball will land based on your partner's movements and strokes. As you both get comfortable with the basic exchanges, increase the pace and incorporate more spin into your shots to simulate real-match scenarios. This drill enhances your ability to control the ball under pressure and improves your reaction times, making you adept at handling unexpected shots during games. It's also fun because it feels like real gameplay.

Volley-to-Volley Practice

The volley-to-volley exchange is a fast-paced drill that sharpens your reflexes and improves your net play coordination.

- Both you and your partner take positions at their respective non-volley line.
- Start a volley exchange, trying to keep the ball going back and forth as long as possible, using only volleys.

This drill requires quick reflexes and precise paddle control, as the rapid exchanges don't allow much time for adjustments. It's an effective way to practice your net game, teaching you to react swiftly and accurately. Volley-to-volley exchanges not only boost your ability to manage fast-paced shots but also enhance your strategic thinking about when and where to place your volleys for optimal advantage.

Cooperative Dinking Drills

Dinking is a skillful part of pickleball that involves strategic, soft shots that land in the opponent's non-volley zone. Practicing dinks with a partner can significantly improve your placement and control.

- Both players stand at their respective non-volley zone lines.
- Take turns hitting soft dinks over the net.
- Focus on keeping the ball within the non-volley zone and try to maintain a rally.

This drill allows players to refine their soft-hand techniques, enhancing their ability to execute gentle shots that are difficult for opponents to return. It's also a great way to develop patience and precision in your play, as effective dinking is about placing the ball just right, rather than overpowering your opponent.

Power Shot Exchanges

To build your ability to handle high-pressure situations, practicing power shot exchanges with your partner can be invaluable.

- Stand at opposite baselines as your partner.
- Practice hitting strong, deep shots to each other.
- Focus on maintaining control of powerful returns and improving your reaction time.

- As the drill progresses, try to increase the speed and power of your shots gradually, which tests both your offensive skills and defensive reactions.
- You can also start with a slow-paced dinking rally, and then have one player randomly speed up the pace with a power shot. This drill helps you learn the transition from a soft game to a hard game.

Power shot exchanges are crucial for developing resilience on the court, training you to stay calm and responsive even when faced with aggressive play from your opponents (Shop the Courts n.d.).

Through these partner drills, you not only sharpen your individual skills but also learn to move, react, and think as a unit. The synergy developed from such practices can make all the difference in matches, where coordination and mutual understanding can turn challenging rallies into winning points. Engaging regularly in these drills with your partner will not only make your practice sessions more enjoyable but also more productive, setting you both up for success in your pickleball endeavors.

TEAM PRACTICES: ENGAGING GROUP DRILLS

One of the funniest ways to practice pickleball is in a team. The camaraderie and collective focus on improvement make these sessions not just beneficial but also incredibly enjoyable.

Rotating Partners

To make the most out of these gatherings, setting up rotational games is a fantastic strategy. These games involve players rotating partners after every game or point, depending on the rules you set. This format not only spices up the practice with variety but also challenges you to adapt to different playing styles and strategies. For instance, playing with a more defensive partner might encourage you to be more aggressive, honing your offensive skills. Conversely, an aggressive partner might push you to tighten your defensive plays. This adaptability is crucial during tournaments where quick strategizing against diverse opponents can lead to victory.

Mini-Tournaments

Another dynamic way to enhance skills in a group setting is through the organization of mini-tournaments. These can be structured to reflect actual match conditions, complete with bracket setups and varying levels of competitive pressure. Mini-tournaments are particularly effective for simulating the mental and physical atmosphere of official games, helping you and your teammates practice endurance and strategic flexibility under pressure. For example, adjusting your gameplay to counter an opponent's unexpected tactics can be practiced here. These tournaments also encourage a healthy, competitive spirit among players, pushing everyone to elevate their game while still in a supportive environment.

Drilling the Soft Game

- All four players stand at the non-volley line.
- The players must practice a soft game, where the ball can only be hit into the non-volley zone.
- Once a mistake is made by hitting the ball into the net or out of the non-volley zone, the players will rotate positions. As a result, the players practice their soft game from all positions on the court and can practice both straight dinks and cross-court dinks.
- You can make things more interesting with the "Crazy 8" technique. Here, two players will always hit the ball straight and two players will always hit the ball cross-court. When someone yells "switch," the players that were hitting straight ahead now hit cross-court, and those that were hitting cross-court will now hit straight ahead.

Drilling the Middle Ground

- Simulate normal match positions.
- The players must aim to drive the ball down the center of the court, where it isn't clear who should return the ball.
- This will teach players to communicate clearly with each other about how best to move to hit the balls that fly down the middle court (Noel 2021).

Through these engaging group drills, team practices can transform from routine gatherings to sessions that dramatically elevate everyone's game, ensuring you and your teammates are not only prepared for official matches but are also continuously finding joy and challenge in the journey of improving together. Engaging in these practices regularly helps build a cohesive team dynamic where each player's improvements contribute to the collective success, making every practice session a step forward for all involved.

USING TECHNOLOGY: APPS AND TOOLS FOR BETTER PRACTICE

We're living in a modern era with a plethora of technological developments. Even though pickleball is a physical sport, it'd be silly to not take advantage of these technological tools. Embracing tech tools can enhance your practice sessions, refine your techniques, and keep you engaged through interactive and measurable methods. Let's explore how various technological solutions, from video analysis tools to wearable fitness trackers, can revolutionize the way you train and play pickleball.

Video Analysis

One of the most effective ways to improve your pickleball skills is through video. Simply set up your mobile phone and record your gameplay, or ask a friend or family member to film it for you. By watching replays of your matches or practice sessions, you can pinpoint specific areas of your technique that need improvement, such as your footwork, paddle positioning, or shot timing.

Advanced software like Dartfish and Coach's Eye even offer features that enable you to annotate videos, draw lines to check body alignment, and even compare your movements side-by-side with professional players or your previous videos. This visual feedback is invaluable as it provides a clear, objective view of your performance, helping you understand and implement technical adjustments more effectively. Moreover, many of these tools are user-friendly and accessible, meaning you can start incorporating them into your practice routine without needing extensive technical knowledge.

Mobile Training Apps

The convenience of mobile training apps has made them a favorite among pickleball enthusiasts. These apps serve as your virtual coach, offering a range of features from skill-building exercises to customized practice routines. Apps like Pickleball Tutor feature modules that focus on specific skills such as serving, volleying, or strategic gameplay. They provide step-by-step instructions, demonstration videos, and even interactive challenges that make your training sessions more engaging and productive. Additionally, some apps, like Pickleball Playbook, allow you to set personal goals and track your progress over time, giving you a clear sense of how your skills are improving. This not only keeps your practice sessions structured but also motivates you by showing tangible progress in your abilities. Other apps, like Pickeplay, are community apps that help you find courts, events, and clubs that match your skill set.

Wearable Fitness Trackers

Wearable technology has transformed how athletes train, and pickleball players can greatly benefit from these devices.

Fitness trackers like Fitbit or Garmin devices are equipped to monitor various physical metrics such as heart rate, calories burned, and activity levels during your practice sessions. More advanced models can even offer analyses of your speed and agility, providing insights into your physical performance on the court. This data is very helpful for understanding your physical strengths and limitations. For instance, tracking your heart rate during different drills can help you gauge your endurance levels and determine whether you need to increase your cardiovascular training. Moreover, these devices often come with apps that allow you to review your performance data over time, enabling you to tailor your fitness routines to better meet the physical demands of pickleball.

Online Coaching Sessions

The availability of online coaching has opened new doors for pickleball players seeking professional guidance. Virtual clinics and coaching sessions connect you with experienced coaches and players from around the world, offering personalized feedback and training advice without the need for physical presence. These sessions can be particularly beneficial if you live in an area with limited access to local pickleball clubs or coaches. Through live video interactions, you can receive real-time feedback on your playing techniques, ask questions, and even participate in live drill demonstrations. Many platforms also offer recorded sessions, allowing you to revisit the lessons at your convenience and practice at your own pace. This flexibility makes it easier to fit training into your schedule, ensuring you continue to improve regardless of your circumstances.

As you integrate these technological tools into your pickleball training regimen, you'll likely notice a significant enhancement in both your skills and your overall approach to the game. Technology not only makes learning and practice more accessible and effective but also adds an element of fun and innovation to your training routine, keeping you motivated and eager to hit the court and test your improved skills.

CREATING A PERSONAL PRACTICE SCHEDULE

Developing a personal practice schedule that caters to your unique needs and goals in pickleball is not just about dedicating time to hit the court; it's about crafting a balanced routine that enhances your skills while also protecting your body and mind. Creating a schedule can keep you focused by providing a visual reminder of your goals and the milestones that you hit along the way.

1. **Assess your personal goals.** Reflect on what you aim to achieve: Are you looking to improve your serve, enhance your volley skills, or prepare for a tournament? Perhaps your goals are more fitness-oriented, aiming to increase your agility and endurance. Recognizing these objectives allows you to tailor your practice sessions to be both focused and productive.
2. **List your strengths and weaknesses as they stand today.** This honest appraisal helps in setting realistic and measurable goals. You can tailor your practice to your specific needs.

3. **Determine how to improve your weaknesses.** What are the key movement patterns involved in the skill? Are you struggling because of your flexibility, strength, endurance, or just a lack of technique?
4. **Establish clear, achievable goals.** Break your big goal down into smaller parts. If you want to win a tournament at the end of the year, what do you need to do to achieve this? You might set the goal to practice three days a week until the tournament.
5. **Design a balanced practice schedule.** This schedule should encompass both technical skills and physical conditioning. Divide your practice time accordingly. For example, dedicate certain days to skill development, focusing on drills that improve your serve, dink, or power shot, while other days might focus on physical conditioning, incorporating activities like cardiovascular workouts or strength training sessions. This variety not only keeps your routine engaging but also ensures a holistic approach to your development as a pickleball player, reducing the risk of overtraining any single aspect of your game.
6. **Incorporate adequate rest.** Rest days are essential for allowing your muscles to recover and grow stronger. Neglecting this can lead to burnout and injuries, which could sideline you from the game you enjoy. Consider integrating active recovery days, where instead of engaging in intense pickleball drills, you might focus on light activities such as walking or yoga. This approach helps maintain your physical activity without overstraining your body, ensuring

that you remain in top form both physically and mentally (Rothermel 2019).

Flexibility in your practice schedule is equally important. Life's unpredictability means that sticking rigidly to a planned routine might not always be possible. Allow yourself the flexibility to adjust your practice sessions based on your daily energy levels and external commitments. If you planned a high-intensity drill session but feel too drained, it might be more beneficial to switch to a strategy review or a light play day. Listening to your body and being adaptable helps maintain a sustainable and enjoyable practice routine, which is essential for long-term engagement with pickleball.

MEASURING PROGRESS: TRACKING SKILLS AND IMPROVEMENT

Tracking General Fitness

The goal of every athlete is to be improving in their gameplay as they gain experience in their sport. Sometimes, it is easiest to track general fitness metrics as indicators that you're in peak condition. The most obvious fitness metric is body weight. As you train pickleball and maintain a healthy diet, your body will begin to transform into peak condition. Otherwise, if your body is not fit for the physicality of the sport, you'll find your performance suffering. You can also use performance tests to track your health improvement. These tests include:

- vertical jump test
- sprint test
- endurance test
- medicine ball throw
- change of direction speed tests.

Tracking Specific Skills

Apart from measuring your general fitness, you can also track your improvement in specific skills. One of the most effective ways to gauge your growth is by establishing clear baselines for your skills at the outset of your training period. Think of this as setting the starting line in a race—it marks where you begin and helps you measure just how far you've come over time. To start, choose several key skills you want to track, such as serve accuracy, volley consistency, or stamina on the court. Record your current ability in each of these areas through quantifiable measures—for instance, how many serves land in the correct box, or how many volleys you can hit without error during a drill. This initial evaluation provides you with a clear, objective set of data against which you can measure future progress.

Regular skill assessments are crucial to this process. They serve as checkpoints along your training path, giving you insight into which areas of your game have improved and which still need attention. These assessments should be conducted in a consistent manner—for example, every month or after every 10 practice sessions. During each assessment, replicate the conditions of your baseline measurements as closely as possible to ensure accuracy. If you originally tested how many serves out of 50 landed in the correct service box, use the same drill to assess your progress. For an even more detailed analysis, consider involving a coach who can provide professional observations and insights, adding depth to your understanding of your skill development.

Keeping a practice journal can transform this tracking process from a mere exercise in data collection into a powerful tool for reflection and motivation. In this journal, record not only the results of your drills and assessments but also how you felt during practice, what challenges you encountered, and how you addressed them. Over time, this journal will become a rich resource, providing insights into your mental and emotional growth alongside your physical improvements. When you face setbacks or feel discouraged, looking back over your journal can remind you of the challenges you've overcome and the progress you've made, rekindling your motivation and commitment to improvement.

Outside Input

Finally, the role of feedback in this process cannot be overstated. Coaches are there to guide you to perform at the highest level. Try to get their professional opinion about your progress, strengths, and weaknesses. If you don't have access to a coach, ask your peers to watch you for 10 minutes. This feedback should form a continuous loop, where the insights you gain are regularly incorporated into your practice strategies. After receiving feedback, adjust your drills and focus areas accordingly, then reassess your skills to see how these adjustments have impacted your performance. This dynamic approach ensures that your practice remains responsive to your evolving needs, keeping you on the most effective path toward your goals (Paula 2020).

Through these methods—tracking general fitness, tracking specific skills, and seeking external feedback—you create a comprehensive and responsive framework for tracking your progress in pickleball. This structured approach not only clarifies your growth trajectory but also deepens your engagement with every aspect of your development, from physical skills to strategic understanding and mental resilience. As you continue to track and reflect on your improvements, you'll find that each step forward is not just about becoming a better player but also about enjoying the game more fully and understanding your journey within it.

As this chapter closes, remember that each practice session is an opportunity to gather data, reflect on achievements, and refine strategies. The insights gained here are not just about improving your game; they're about enriching your entire pickleball experience, making each match more enjoyable and each victory more rewarding. With your progress now measurable and your goals clearer, the next chapter will guide you in leveraging community resources and events to further enrich your pickleball journey, connecting your personal improvements to the broader world of pickleball play and culture.

THE SOCIAL AND COMMUNITY ASPECT OF PICKLEBALL

Pickleball is a social game for a reason. A great team can make all the difference in your playing experience. This chapter is dedicated to exploring how you can immerse yourself in the pickleball community, starting with finding and joining clubs and leagues that match your interests and skill level. Next, we give a step-by-step guide to hosting your own tournament.

From here, we look at how pickleball can be played by anyone in the family. We give some tips on how to avoid family spats, encourage kids to participate, and get the seniors involved. Finally, we look at how you can use social media to expand your pickleball network. Whether you are looking to make new friends, get some quality family time, improve your game, or simply enjoy the social atmosphere, understanding how to navigate the community aspect of pickleball is key.

FINDING AND JOINING PICKLEBALL CLUBS AND LEAGUES

Researching Local Options

Embarking on your pickleball journey begins with finding where the players are. Let's look at the best ways to find pickleball courts near you:

- **Use a simple online search.** Your search engine will recommend nearby courts so that you can see all your options for play.
- **Take advantage of the apps.** Places2Play and PicklePlay are both great apps that allow you to stay informed about pickleball courts, tournaments, and more. Both of these apps are free and can be used through their website or mobile app.
- **Use a directory.** Websites like the USA Pickleball Association offer directories of local clubs that provide a wealth of information, including club size, location, and playing times.
- **Turn to social media.** Many clubs and community groups maintain active social media pages where they post updates on event schedules, open play times, and membership details. These platforms also allow you to see comments and photos from current members, which can give you a sense of the club's atmosphere and community spirit.
- **Check your local community centers.** Community bulletin boards in local gyms, community centers, and sports stores are always worth checking. Often,

local pickleball groups will post flyers and announcements in these high-traffic areas to attract new members.
- **Make your own court.** If all else fails and you can't find a suitable court nearby, you can create a temporary court at home. All you need is a portable net, some paddles, balls, and some tape to mark out your lines. Invite your family and friends around and create your own pickleball community (Paddletek n.d.-e)!

By combining these resources, you can compile a comprehensive list of potential clubs and leagues near you, giving you a solid starting point for deeper exploration.

Evaluating Fit

Once you have identified a few potential clubs or leagues, the next step is evaluating if they're a good fit for you.

- **Consider your skill level.** Some clubs might be geared more toward competitive play, while others may focus on recreational or beginner-friendly games. Attending a few open play sessions can give you firsthand experience of the pace and style of play, helping you determine if it matches your abilities and goals.
- **Consider the social atmosphere.** Are you looking for a highly social group where players often gather after games or a more game-focused club? Observing or participating in a session can help you gauge the social dynamics of the group.

- **Consider the location and schedule of the club's activities.** Ensure that the meeting times and venues are convenient for you, to make regular attendance feasible without disrupting your daily routine.
- **Consider the membership benefits.** Joining a pickleball club or league comes with numerous benefits. Many clubs provide access to coaching and skill development clinics, which can be invaluable for improving your technique and strategy. Moreover, any social events organized by these clubs foster a sense of community and belonging.
- **Try out a few options.** Where do you have the most fun? Pickleball is all about making new friends, so make sure you choose somewhere that you fit in well.

First Steps to Joining

Taking the first step to join can sometimes be daunting, but it's simpler than you might think. Remember, everyone started where you are now. Just follow these simple steps to join your first club.

1. Start by reaching out to the club organizer or attending an open play session.
2. Introduce yourself to a few members and express your interest in joining. Be open about your skill level and your reasons for wanting to join; this honesty will help members guide you to the most suitable play groups.
3. Ensure you understand any membership fees or commitments. Many clubs have very reasonable fees

and flexible attendance rules, but it's important to be clear about these details upfront.
4. Lastly, make a positive impression by showing enthusiasm and respect for the club's rules and culture. A friendly attitude and a readiness to engage not only enrich your entry into the club but also set the stage for a rewarding pickleball experience.

By taking these steps, you can smoothly integrate into a pickleball community. This will be the exciting beginning of better gameplay and new friends. The connections you make through pickleball can extend beyond the court, adding a valuable layer of support to your life.

HOSTING PICKLEBALL EVENTS AND TOURNAMENTS

Organizing a pickleball event or tournament can be a thrilling way to bring friends, family, and fellow players together. You can showcase your skills and strengthen community ties. Whether you're planning a small tournament at a local park or a larger event at a dedicated club, there are several components that need to be organized. Let's walk through the essential steps required to plan and execute a memorable pickleball event that everyone will love.

1. **Define your tournament type.** There are several common tournament formats, including round-robin, single-elimination, and double-elimination. Will your tournament be playing singles or doubles? Make sure you consider the expected number of participants and their skill level.

2. **Pick your venue.** The venue must accommodate the number of courts needed for the number of participants expected. Consider factors like parking, restroom facilities, and accessibility. Community centers, local parks, or sports clubs often have the necessary amenities and enough space to host such events.
3. **Choose a date.** Choose a date that avoids major holidays and consider the local climate to ensure optimal playing conditions. Early morning start times can help avoid the midday heat, especially during warmer seasons. Don't plan your tournament during the rainiest month of the year.
4. **Promote your event.** Create eye-catching flyers and posters to distribute in local sports centers, community bulletin boards, and pickleball clubs. Use online platforms to broaden your reach; set up an event page on Facebook or use event management platforms like Eventbrite, which can handle invitations, registrations, and even ticket sales if your event is on a larger scale. Regular social media posts leading up to the event can generate excitement and keep the tournament in potential attendees' minds. You could even create a unique hashtag for your event to help spread the word and make it easy for people to share related content. Provide clear information on how to sign up, the cost involved, the categories available (e.g., singles, doubles, mixed doubles), and any rules or formats specific to your tournament.
5. **Organize your equipment.** Ensure there are enough pickleball paddles, balls, and nets for all participants.

It's also wise to have first aid kits, water coolers, and perhaps even tents or shelters for players and spectators. If your event is larger or if you expect a significant audience, consider amenities like seating and refreshments. For a large event, you can engage with local sports shops or pickleball equipment suppliers who might be willing to sponsor your event by providing equipment in exchange for advertising opportunities.

6. **Schedule your matches.** Plan your tournament schedule, including match times, court assignments, and brackets. Make sure that you allow enough time for players to warm up and give them sufficient breaks between matches.
7. **Determine how to officiate the matches.** For smaller events, you may choose to have players self-officiate. You can also recruit volunteer referees. It's helpful to have volunteers or staff members who know the rules of pickleball and can oversee the matches to ensure fair play and handle any disputes that arise.
8. **Keep track of the scores.** Keeping track of scores and match progress is essential, especially for larger tournaments. Design a system for recording the match results. A smaller tournament might use a whiteboard. A larger tournament could consider using digital tools or apps designed for tournament management, which can help update brackets in real time and keep participants informed about when and where they are playing.
9. **Celebrate the winners.** Don't overlook the importance of an awards ceremony. It's a chance to

celebrate the winners, thank everyone for their participation, and possibly even highlight sponsors or significant contributors. You should recognize sportsmanship as well as skill. Prepare in advance by having medals, trophies, or other prizes ready to be awarded at the end of the tournament.
10. **Capture the memories.** Assign someone to take videos and photos of the tournament on the day. Gathering and sharing photos or videos of the tournament can keep the enthusiasm going long after the nets are packed away. Post highlights on social media or the event page to keep the community engaged and excited for your next event. This not only keeps the existing community connected but can also attract new participants who see the fun and camaraderie experienced at your event.
11. **Ask for feedback.** After the tournament, send participants a feedback survey asking for input on what went well and what could be improved. This information is invaluable for planning your next event (Frazier 2024).

BUILDING A PICKLEBALL COMMUNITY: TIPS AND STRATEGIES

Building a thriving pickleball community involves more than just playing the game; it's about creating a welcoming, inclusive environment that fosters long-term engagement and growth. Here are a few ways that you can boost engagement in your pickleball community to build stronger social ties.

- **Have regular social gatherings.** These can range from casual post-game coffee meetups to organized social events like picnics or potlucks. These gatherings are crucial as they provide an opportunity for members to bond beyond the courts, sharing stories, strategies, and even personal milestones. Engaging in activities unrelated to pickleball during these gatherings can also help to strengthen the community bonds, as it allows members to see different facets of each other's personalities and lives, enhancing mutual respect and camaraderie.
- **Host workshops.** These can cover a variety of topics relevant to both new and experienced players, such as tips for improving gameplay, strategies for doubles, nutrition, and fitness for athletes, or even mental toughness training. Bringing in experienced coaches or experts for these workshops can provide valuable insights and learning opportunities for the community. Furthermore, organizing volunteer opportunities related to pickleball, such as charity tournaments or coaching sessions for local schools, can not only bring the community together but also promote the sport and its values to a wider audience. These activities underscore the community's commitment to growth and outreach, fostering a sense of pride and collective purpose among its members.
- **Foster inclusivity.** This means actively ensuring that new members feel welcomed and valued, regardless of their skill level, background, or age. Consider implementing mentorship programs where more experienced players are paired with newcomers to

guide them through the rules of the game, share tips, and provide general support. This not only helps new members acclimate more quickly but also builds a sense of belonging and loyalty to the community. Additionally, be mindful of language and activities that are inclusive; for instance, using gender-neutral terms and ensuring that events are accessible to people with disabilities. Creating a community where everyone feels respected and valued not only enhances individual experiences but also solidifies the community's reputation as a welcoming and diverse group.

- **Consider partnering with local businesses, schools, and other organizations.** This can be incredibly beneficial in supporting and expanding community activities. For example, local sports shops might be interested in sponsoring tournaments in exchange for advertising their products, while schools might welcome partnerships that introduce pickleball to their students, helping to nurture a new generation of players. These collaborations can provide financial support or resources that are necessary for hosting events or expanding facilities. Moreover, they can increase the visibility of pickleball in the community, attracting more participants and creating additional growth opportunities. When approaching potential partners or sponsors, it's important to clearly articulate the benefits of their involvement, such as increased brand exposure or the chance to be associated with a healthy, community-focused activity.

- **Look at a leadership committee.** Consider establishing a community board or leadership team responsible for organizing events, managing finances, and guiding the community's development. Enthusiastic players are often willing to be on these committees on a volunteer basis. Implementing structured feedback systems, like group meetings, where members can voice their opinions and suggest improvements, can also help in adapting to changing needs and preferences, keeping the community dynamic and responsive. Regularly setting goals for community growth, such as increasing membership numbers, expanding facilities, or enhancing member engagement, and revisiting these goals can provide clear direction and motivation for all members involved.

By focusing on these strategies—enhancing social connections, ensuring inclusivity, forging partnerships, and developing leadership—you can build a pickleball community that is not only vibrant and engaging but also resilient and enduring. This kind of community not only supports its members but also contributes significantly to the broader growth and popularity of pickleball as a sport.

PICKLEBALL FOR ALL AGES: ENGAGING DIFFERENT GENERATIONS

Pickleball, with its adaptable and accessible nature, is especially great at engaging individuals across all age groups. This sport has an amazing way of creating a bridge between generations. This inclusivity not only enriches the experience but also fosters a broader sense of community and understanding among players of mixed ages. Let's explore various strategies to involve everyone from the youngest enthusiasts to senior players, ensuring that pickleball remains a sport for all.

Family-Friendly Activities

Pickleball is one of my favorite things to do as a family. On holidays, my family will spend hours and hours on the pickleball court. Because it is so fun and accessible, any member of the family can play it. Even our friends who don't normally play sports always end up having a good time on the court with us!

However, I come from a pretty competitive family. I'm sure a lot of you do, too. As a result, tensions can get quite high on the court. Here are a few tips to help you avoid turning your family bonding into a family feud:

- **Understand what type of game you are playing.** Are you having a social game where you're introducing someone to the rules for the first time? Or are you playing a competitive match against your rival friends?
- **Check your force.** If everyone's skill levels are equal, then it's fun to give your 100% effort and play hard for the win. But, if you're at a higher level than your family, there's no benefit to playing so hard that you humiliate them.

- **Designate a referee.** For my family, this is always my Nana because she can't play anymore. This person can call any faults and scores, to avoid any spats between players.
- **Speak kindly to each other.** If you start making sarcastic or rude comments over the game, you'll likely keep this attitude for the rest of the day. This goes for body language, too—don't roll your eyes, throw up your hands, or sigh at your partner's mistakes. If you don't have anything nice to say, don't say anything at all (Grissom 2024)!

If you have a large family, then you can organize family play days. These events can be themed to make them more exciting, like having a retro day where families come dressed in vintage sports gear, or a superhero day, especially appealing to younger children. During these events, consider modifying the rules to accommodate younger players.

Beyond just playing pickleball, these family days can include other fun activities such as skill contests, where families compete in friendly challenges like "longest rally" or "most accurate serve." Introducing a picnic or barbecue segment can turn the day into a social event, encouraging families to relax and mingle, strengthening your bonds. These gatherings not only make the sport a fun and engaging family activity but also instill a love for pickleball in the younger generation, ensuring the sport's growth and continuity.

Senior Engagement

Age is just a number, especially in pickleball. Pickleball is extremely popular among seniors. It's not too strenuous but not too relaxed—the perfect sport for seniors wanting a bit of physical activity, mental stimulation, and social engagement.

For older adults, engaging in pickleball can promote physical health, such as enhancing coordination, balance, and flexibility; encouraging cognitive sharpness through strategy and shot decision-making; and boosting mental well-being by reducing feelings of isolation and depression. Because pickleball is such a low-impact sport, it is the perfect fit for seniors.

Of course, seniors have a slightly higher risk of injury than younger players. But this risk is easily mitigated. Make sure that you take the time to warm up correctly and get a good grasp of the technique. Knowing how to move, swing, and position yourself on the court can prevent the jarring movements that could lead to sprains or strains.

To cater to older seniors who are starting to slow down, special clinics can be organized that focus on skills and strategies suitable for their physical capabilities. These clinics should emphasize gentle movements and balance exercises to prevent injuries and also highlight the social aspects of the game to encourage participation. You can also easily modify pickleball if it becomes too strenuous for any seniors. Options like using lighter balls, lower nets, and even allowing a second bounce can make the game more enjoyable and less strenuous for older players (Paddletek n.d.-f).

Youth Programs

Pickleball is also an amazing game for kids, due to its simple rules, compact court size, and slower pace. Here are some tips to help you get your kids involved in pickleball:

- **Help them learn the basics.** Familiarize your kids with the rules, scoring system, and where to stand. It can be helpful to have three kids play with one adult who knows the rules and can lead the game.
- **Find the right equipment.** You don't need smaller pickleball paddles unless the kids are toddlers. A regulation-sized paddle will be fine for anyone. Make sure the kids are wearing proper athletic shoes. Nobody should be playing in sandals or barefoot because it increases their risk of injury.
- **Start with mini-games.** You can begin with mini-games or modified versions of pickleball, like some of the drills mentioned in chapter six. You can simply get the kids to rally back and forth for as long as they can. Gradually introduce them to the rules as they gain confidence and skill.
- **Consider enrolling them in pickleball programs.** Many community centers and sports clubs offer pickleball lessons or camps designed for kids. These programs will focus not only on teaching the fundamental skills of the game but also on making the learning process fun and engaging.
- **Enter them in competitions and events.** Organizing regular mini-tournaments or league play can give young players something to strive for and help them experience the thrill of competition.

Rewards or recognition, such as certificates, medals, or gear, can add to the incentive. It's important to foster a supportive environment where the focus is on effort and improvement rather than just winning. This approach not only improves skills but also builds confidence and sportsmanship (Zhuo 2023).

Cross-Generation Interaction

Fostering interactions between different generations through pickleball can lead to an enriched experience for all involved. Mixed-age matches, where teams are composed of younger and older players, can be particularly effective. These settings allow younger players to learn from the experience and tactical knowledge of older players, while the older participants can benefit from the energy and enthusiasm of the younger ones.

Organizing mentorship programs within the club can also be beneficial. Pairing a senior member with a junior player allows mentors to help transfer knowledge, skills, and passion for the game across generations. Additionally, consider hosting skill-sharing workshops where players from different age groups demonstrate and teach their favorite pickleball techniques or strategies. These activities not only improve players' skills but also foster respect, understanding, and camaraderie among them.

By embracing these strategies, pickleball clubs and communities can create a vibrant, multigenerational environment where everyone feels valued and engaged. Through thoughtful programming and inclusive activities, pickleball can continue to be a sport that not only bridges generations but also brings them together. This really is a sport for everyone!

THE ROLE OF SOCIAL MEDIA IN GROWING YOUR PICKLEBALL NETWORK

Social media is a fantastic way to expand your pickleball community. Here are some tips to create a social platform and grow your pickleball network.

- **Choose your platform.** Each social media platform caters to different demographics and offers unique tools for engagement. For instance, Facebook is excellent for reaching a broad audience, including older adults (one of the fastest-growing demographics in pickleball.) It allows for the creation of dedicated groups where members can post schedules, share photos, and coordinate events. Instagram, with its visual-centric format, appeals to a younger audience and is ideal for sharing dynamic content such as videos from tournaments, photo highlights from events, and visual stories that showcase the energy and excitement of pickleball. For real-time interaction and updates, X (formerly Twitter) can be a powerful tool to keep your community informed and engaged with quick posts, links to registration pages, or live updates during events. YouTube is used for detailed instructional videos or testimonials and can provide an in-depth look at your community's activities and benefits, attracting those interested in learning more about pickleball.

- **Take notes from those who have already succeeded.** There are already some great pickleball influencers who you can take inspiration from. Take a look at "Pickleball Barbie," Sydney Stienaker, who has over 55,000 followers on TikTok. Award-winning pickleball player and coach Michele is on Instagram as @thepickleyogi, and is easily one of the most popular pickleball influencers. Shea Underwood is one of the most popular male pickleball influencers, with over 25,000 TikTok followers. Check out their content, because you can always learn from other people's success (IZEA 2023).
- **Create interesting content.** Start with content that educates and informs. How-to videos, tips for improving gameplay, and explanations of rules can be incredibly beneficial for new players. Highlighting community achievements, such as tournament results or milestones in membership growth, helps build a narrative of success and progression that can attract new members and sponsors. Consider featuring member stories or spotlight posts that focus on individual achievements or experiences within the community. These personal stories can resonate deeply, fostering a sense of connection and community spirit.
- **Interact with the community.** Regularly respond to your comments and messages. Hosting live Q&A sessions with pickleball experts or coaches can offer direct interaction and valuable learning opportunities for your members. Encourage members to share their own stories and experiences

or to contribute tips and advice in community group chats or forums. This not only enriches the community's knowledge base but also empowers members by giving them a voice within the community.

- **Organize virtual events.** Online meetups, webinars on strategy or fitness, or virtual watch parties for major pickleball tournaments can provide additional opportunities for engagement, especially for members who may not always be able to attend in-person events. These activities help maintain an active and engaged community, crucial for its growth and sustainability.
- **Monitor your engagement.** Most social media platforms provide analytics tools that allow you to track metrics such as likes, shares, comments, views, and the reach of your posts. Analyzing these metrics helps you understand what types of content resonate most with your audience, allowing you to tailor your strategy to better meet their interests and needs. Tracking engagement over time can also help identify trends, such as increased interest in specific types of posts or activities, or fluctuations in engagement that could indicate the need for adjustments in your strategy. Additionally, monitoring feedback and engagement can provide insights into the community's perceptions and opinions, which can be invaluable for adapting and enhancing community experiences and offerings.

By strategically utilizing social media to engage with and grow your pickleball network, you can not only enhance the visibility and attractiveness of your community but also create a dynamic, interactive platform that fosters stronger connections and a more vibrant community spirit. If your platform grows big enough, you can even monetize your content and start earning some extra money! Whether through thoughtful content creation, interactive engagement strategies, or meticulous monitoring of your social media presence, the potential to expand and enrich your pickleball community through these digital platforms is immense.

As we conclude this chapter on the social and community aspects of pickleball, I hope you can see the immense value in fostering connections that extend beyond the court. From joining clubs to playing with your family, the essence of pickleball is as much about community as it is about the sport itself. As you move forward, remember that every serve, every point, and every game is an opportunity to build relationships and contribute to a sense of community. Let's carry this community spirit into the next chapter, where we explore how you can take your game to the next level by playing competitively in tournaments.

TAKING YOUR GAME TO THE NEXT LEVEL

❦

Now that you're reaching the end of this book, you are firmly set up to be a great pickleball player. You're equipped with all the basic techniques and advanced strategies that have you winning matches left, right, and center. Now, it's time for you to step past the casual back-and-forth of community play and experience the thrill of testing your skills against a broader array of players. It's here, in the thick of competitive play, that you truly get to put your training, strategy, and mental toughness to the test. Whether you're eyeing your first local tournament or setting your sights on broader horizons, this chapter will help you to understand the nuances of professional tournaments.

To begin, we'll give you a step-by-step guide to preparing for your first tournament. Next, we'll look at some game-day strategies that you can use to ensure you're winning your matches. We'll retouch on the mental preparation and focus techniques that can help you play your best game. From here, we'll explain the recommended fitness and nutrition protocols to ensure you're at peak performance for your tournament. Next, we'll clarify pickleball tournament etiquette to help you avoid making any blunders on your big day. To finish, we'll reflect on your pickleball growth and future goals.

PREPARING FOR YOUR FIRST TOURNAMENT

1. **Choose the right tournament.** First, consider your current skill level. Are you a beginner looking to dip your toes into competitive waters, or are you an intermediate player ready to challenge yourself against stronger competitors? Tournaments often have different divisions based on skill level, ensuring that you're matched against similarly skilled players. Location is another critical factor. Local tournaments are a great start because they offer the comfort of familiar surroundings and lower travel demands. As you grow more confident, regional or national tournaments might beckon, offering you a taste of broader competitive scenes and higher-level play dynamics.
2. **Register.** This process usually involves filling out an online form and paying a registration fee. Make sure you understand the classification and division criteria of the tournament to register in the appropriate category that matches your skill level. Misclassification can lead to mismatches that might not be enjoyable or beneficial for your development. Many tournaments also have early registration discounts, so it's advantageous to plan ahead. Keep

an eye on registration deadlines too, as missing these can mean missing out on the opportunity to compete. After registering, you'll typically receive confirmation and a player packet that includes important information such as schedules, rules, and other logistics.
3. **Prepare.** Make sure that you have all the right equipment. Check your paddle for any wear and tear and replace it if necessary. Pack your bag a day before to avoid last-minute rushes which can unsettle your mental preparation. Create a practice schedule leading up to the event that balances skill refinement with physical conditioning. If possible, try to learn about your potential opponents. Many players have match videos available online and studying these can offer insights into their playing style and strategies, which you can practice against. This scouting can give you a tactical edge, allowing you to enter the tournament with strategies already tailored to counter specific opponents.
4. **Get there early.** Aim to get there early to acclimatize yourself to the environment. Locate essential areas such as the check-in desk, restrooms, and the courts where you'll be playing. Warming up is crucial, not just physically but also to get a feel for the playing conditions, which can vary significantly from what you're used to.
5. **Manage your energy throughout the day.** Tournaments often involve waiting periods between matches, so bring something to keep you relaxed and occupied during these times. Stay hydrated and have snacks ready to maintain your energy levels. Most

importantly, keep a positive mindset. Focus on each point and each game at a time, and remember why you started playing pickleball—to challenge yourself, enjoy the competition, and continuously improve.

With these strategies and preparations in place, you're maximizing your opportunity to grow, learn, and excel in the competitive arena of pickleball. Each match is a step forward in your playing career, irrespective of the immediate outcome. Embrace the challenge, enjoy the experience, and take your game to the next level.

ADVANCED COMPETITIVE STRATEGIES

When stepping into a pickleball tournament, your strategic preparation can be as critical as your physical readiness.

- **Analyze your opponent.** Observing and understanding their strengths, weaknesses, and playing styles can provide you with crucial insights that allow you to tailor your strategies in a way that maximizes your chances of success. Begin by watching previous matches of your opponents, if possible. Otherwise, see what you can pick up as you're versing them on the court. Pay attention to their preferred shots, their movement on the court, and how they react under pressure. Do they favor a powerful forehand? Are they uncomfortable with backhand shots? Do they prefer a soft game with lots of dinks or a hard game with power shots? Knowing these details can help you plan your plays, targeting their vulnerabilities and avoiding their strengths.

- **Adapt your gameplay.** The ability to modify your strategy based on the ongoing dynamics of the match is invaluable. This flexibility might involve changing your serving strategy, adjusting your positioning on the court, or even altering your defensive tactics to disrupt your opponent's rhythm. For instance, if you notice your opponent is struggling with returning deep serves, you might choose to focus on this strategy until they adapt, at which point you might switch to shorter, more angled serves to keep them off-balance. This kind of adaptability requires a good understanding of pickleball strategies and an ability to remain mentally flexible and composed under pressure.
- **Incorporate specialized shots into your gameplay.** If you have some more advanced shots in your arsenal, use them! The spin serve, for instance, can add an unpredictable element to your service game, making it harder for opponents to predict and return the ball effectively.
- **Remember to communicate in doubles play.** Who is going to cover the middle line? You can assign one player to be more aggressive and handle most of the volleys and smashes, while the other might specialize in defensive plays and accurate placements. Switching formations based on the flow of the game can also confuse opponents and create new angles and opportunities. For example, the traditional side-by-side formation might be switched to a stacked formation, where both players align on one side of the court, to cover the court more effectively and play to each player's strengths. Synchronized

movements, where both players move in harmony, can prevent gaps on the court and present a united front that can be intimidating for opponents to break down.

These strategies and techniques, when mastered and applied thoughtfully, can elevate your playing and significantly boost your performance in competitive settings. The key is to practice these strategies consistently and always remain adaptable to the evolving dynamics of each match. As you integrate these advanced strategies into your play, you'll find yourself not just participating in tournaments, but truly competing to win.

MENTAL TOUGHNESS IN COMPETITIVE PLAY

When the pressure mounts and the stakes are high, the mental game in pickleball becomes as important as physical ability. Developing mental toughness allows you to navigate through setbacks, losses, and high-pressure situations with a mindset geared toward growth and learning. We already covered the best ways to mentally prepare for a game in chapter two, but I'll recap it again for you here.

- **Maintain your focus.** The chaos of a tournament environment, the delays, the cheering crowds, or the multiple matches can easily distract you. If you give your attention to distractions, you will underperform. Before you play, do a mindfulness practice. Set a timer for five minutes and focus on your breathwork. Then, take a few minutes to visualize yourself playing. Imagine yourself

executing all of the perfect shots. During the game, you can ask a refocusing question, like, "What's important now?" to redirect your thoughts to the task at hand. Or, you can repeat a thought-stopping mantra, like, "Let it go; focus on the next play," to help you recenter your mind.
- **Use positive self-talk.** Replace any critical thoughts with affirmations and encouragements. Turn "I can't do this" into "I can do this," "I'm prepared for this," and "I'm here to have fun." This ability to regulate your emotions ensures that they enhance your performance—using the adrenaline rush of excitement to sharpen your focus rather than letting nerves undermine your play.
- **Stay resilient in the face of challenges.** Setbacks are just a part of playing pickleball. View your mistakes as opportunities to learn and improve.
- **There's more to the game than winning.** Techniques such as setting small, achievable goals during matches or focusing on process over outcome help in developing this resilience. For instance, instead of getting bogged down by a loss, you could focus on the number of successful serves or the effective use of a particular strategy. This approach helps maintain a positive outlook and keeps you motivated, turning every match, regardless of its outcome, into a stepping stone toward mastery.
- **Reflect on your performance post-match.** Reflecting on your performance after each match, identifying what went well and what didn't, and thinking strategically about adjustments for future games are all part of this process. This doesn't just

apply to technique but also to your mental and emotional strategies. Did your focus waver? What caused it? How did you handle the pressure of a tight game? Answering these questions can provide valuable insights, which you can then use to refine your approach, both on and off the court. Keeping a journal where you record these reflections can be particularly useful (Straw 2023).

Implementing these mental strategies will leave you well-prepared for the rigors of competitive play. As you continue to compete and implement these mental strategies, you'll find that your ability to handle the pressures of competitive pickleball will grow, allowing you to play not just harder, but smarter.

NUTRITION AND FITNESS FOR PEAK PERFORMANCE

When considering your performance at pickleball tournaments, the role of proper nutrition and a tailored fitness regimen cannot be overstated. The right foods and fluids before, during, and after play can significantly affect your energy levels, concentration, and overall performance, while a targeted fitness approach ensures you have the stamina, strength, and agility needed to compete at your best.

Optimizing Tournament Nutrition

What you eat on the day of a tournament can have a big influence on your performance. Your nutritional strategy for a tournament should address three key phases: before, during, and after the games.

- **Before the Tournament:** Prior to a tournament, your focus should be on building up a reserve of slow-releasing energy. Meals should be rich in complex carbohydrates, which provide the primary fuel for exercising muscles. Pair these carbohydrates with moderate amounts of lean protein and healthy fats, like chicken, and fish, to aid muscle repair and recovery. Aim to have a small meal one to three hours before the game. This will give your body enough time to digest before you play. I recommend having some oatmeal with berries, a bagel, or a sandwich. Make sure that you're completely hydrated; drink lots of water from the day before.
- **During the Tournament:** During the tournament, maintaining energy and hydration levels is paramount. Having food during exercise may result in stomach cramps, but make sure that you're eating during your breaks to keep your energy levels high. Snacks should be easy to digest and primarily carbohydrate-based, like bananas, energy bars, and small sandwiches with peanut butter. Aim to drink at least 16 ounces of water per hour. If the matches are lengthy or it's particularly hot, sports drinks can help replenish electrolytes lost through sweat. Avoid any energy drinks or high-sugar sodas, as these may upset your stomach.
- **After the Tournament:** After the day's play, recovery becomes the focus. During heavy exercise, your body taps into your glycogen storage for energy. The best

thing to do after a game is to eat something with protein and carbohydrates to refuel your energy stores. This meal should be higher in protein to aid muscle recovery. A meal like grilled chicken with quinoa and vegetables, or a hearty fish stew with potatoes, can provide the necessary nutrients to aid recovery. Including anti-inflammatory foods like berries, salmon, and leafy greens can also help reduce any muscle soreness and prepare you for subsequent games or training sessions. The research shows that your body's ability to refill muscle stores decreases by 50 percent if you wait over two hours to eat after your workout. So the sooner you refuel, the better (PT & Me 2023)!

Fitness Regimen for Competitive Players

Developing a fitness regimen that complements your pickleball play enhances your ability to perform well during tournaments. As we discussed in chapter two, you should focus on four main areas: endurance, strength, flexibility, and agility. Dedicate one or two sessions each week to training in each of these areas, and you'll see both your fitness and pickleball ability flourish.

- **Endurance keeps your heart and lungs healthy.** Endurance can be built through cardiovascular activities such as running, cycling, or swimming, which help increase your stamina and improve heart health.
- **Strength training is equally important.** It not only boosts your power during play but also supports

joint health and reduces injury risk. Incorporate exercises that target the core, legs, and arms. If you're not interested in joining a gym, utilizing resistance bands, free weights, or body-weight exercises like squats, lunges, push-ups, and planks can be effective.
- **Flexibility allows you to safely reach and bend for the pickleball.** You can improve your flexibility by dynamically stretching before training, static stretching after training, and doing some yoga or Pilates.
- **Agility training enhances your ability to change direction quickly—an essential skill in pickleball.** Drills that involve lateral movements, quick feet, and changes of direction can improve your agility on the court. Setting up agility ladders or using cones to create drill courses are practical methods to enhance your footwork and speed (Read 2021).

Recovery Protocols

Your recovery is equally as important as your preparation. You need to make sure that you recover properly after a tournament, or you'll probably end up so sore that you can't walk... I've been there. Here are a few techniques to help you recover after a tournament:

- **Stretching:** After each day of play, engage in a cool-down routine that includes gentle stretching to relax muscles and promote flexibility. Focus on stretches that target key muscle groups used in pickleball, such as the calves, hamstrings, shoulders, and back.

- **Active Recovery:** Active recovery often takes the form of a cool-down jog after the games are finished. A recent review found that 6-10 minutes of light aerobic activity can improve how we feel the next day.
- **Foam Rolling:** Foam rolling is a great way to stretch your muscles out and prevent them from being too tender the next day.
- **Ice Baths:** Ice baths are becoming increasingly popular, and for good reason. Multiple strong studies have concluded that ice bathing will reduce soreness after intense exercise. The average length of ice baths is around 13 minutes, so that's a good place to start (Fergus n.d.).

By integrating these nutritional strategies, hydration tips, fitness regimen suggestions, and recovery protocols into your preparation and routine, you equip yourself with a solid foundation to handle the rigors of competitive pickleball. This holistic approach not only prepares your body and mind for the demands of tournament play but also supports your overall health and wellness, allowing you to enjoy and excel in the sport for years to come.

THE ETIQUETTE OF COMPETITIVE PICKLEBALL

When you decide to venture into competitive pickleball, understanding and practicing good sportsmanship is as important as mastering the physical skills of the game. The principles of sportsmanship encompass far more than just adhering to the rules; they involve a respect for fellow players, officials, and the spirit of the game itself.

- **Respect fair play.** This means making honest calls on line shots, serving within the rules, and respecting the decisions of officials, even when they go against you. It also involves acknowledging the good plays made by your opponents and maintaining a positive attitude, whether you are winning or losing. This respect for others ensures that the competitive environment remains friendly and enjoyable for everyone involved.
- **Handle disputes with composure.** Disagreements might arise about game plays or scoring, but try to handle these with grace. If a dispute occurs, give your opponent the benefit of the doubt. We want to play a fun game, so don't sweat the small stuff. If the dispute cannot be resolved between players, a referee or a tournament official should be consulted. They can provide an impartial decision that should be respected by all parties involved
- **Practice court courtesy.** Sometimes, it seems like pickleballs have a mind of their own. They seem to fly anywhere. When a ball from another court rolls onto yours, you need to say a quick "Ball on court!" to alert the other players. Don't throw the ball across a couple of courts to the owner. This might seem efficient, but you could end up hitting someone. Instead, gently roll the ball back. This not only shows respect for the safety of the players but also for the flow of the game. It's also important to minimize interruptions to other games. Enter and exit your court quickly and quietly, especially if other games are in progress. This respect ensures that all players

can enjoy their games without unnecessary distractions.
- **Respect the facilities.** This sounds obvious, but make sure you're keeping the court and its surroundings clean, disposing of trash properly, and taking care of any equipment provided.
- **Respect the officials.** Officials and volunteers play a crucial role in organizing and managing pickleball tournaments. Interacting with them respectfully and appreciatively is essential. Understanding that officials are there to enforce the rules and ensure fair play helps in accepting their decisions gracefully, even if they are unfavorable. During a match, if you disagree with an official's call, it is appropriate to ask for clarification politely, but always respect the final decision. Acknowledging the hard work of volunteers and officials with a simple thank you or other gestures of appreciation fosters a positive atmosphere and encourages a supportive community.
- **Don't be a sore loser or an obnoxious winner.** How you handle both victories and defeats can significantly impact your reputation as a sportsman. Celebrating wins with humility and acknowledging the effort of your opponent shows respect and appreciation for their participation. A simple fist bump or paddle tap is a good way to celebrate. Over-the-top celebrations can be a bit distasteful. On the other hand, accepting losses without negative behavior or excuses is equally important. Viewing losses as opportunities to learn and improve not only helps you grow as a player but also contributes to a

supportive environment where players feel valued and motivated (Paddletek n.d.-d).

In essence, embracing the etiquette of competitive pickleplay enriches the experience for everyone involved. It builds a community where competition can thrive without sacrificing respect or enjoyment. Whether you're stepping onto the court for a local tournament or a national competition, these principles of sportsmanship and etiquette guide your interactions, ensuring that the spirit of pickleball remains positive and inclusive.

REFLECTING ON YOUR PICKLEBALL JOURNEY: GROWTH AND GOALS

Once you start playing competitively, it becomes increasingly valuable to set long-term goals that align with your aspirations in the sport. These goals could range from improving specific technical skills or winning a particular tournament to simply enhancing your enjoyment of the game. Setting clear, achievable goals not only provides direction to your training efforts but also injects motivation and purpose into your pickleball practice. Start by identifying what aspects of pickleball you are most passionate about or areas where you feel improvement would be most satisfying. Is it mastering a powerful serve, excelling in doubles play, or perhaps just becoming more consistent in your game? Once these areas are identified, set specific, measurable objectives that can guide your efforts. For example, if improving your serve is a goal, you might aim to increase your service ace count in games or achieve a higher percentage of successful first serves during practice sessions.

Tracking your progress toward these goals will provide feedback on your development and help maintain your motivation. One effective method is maintaining a play diary where you record outcomes of games, personal performance metrics, and observations on what tactics worked or didn't work. This diary can be a valuable resource for identifying patterns in your play that may be contributing to your successes or hindrances. Additionally, you can record your matches to see any insights that are not perceivable during gameplay. Reviewing these recordings with a coach or a more experienced player can help pinpoint areas that need improvement or adjustment.

Another aspect of your growth in pickleball involves continuous learning and development. The sport is always evolving, with new strategies, techniques, and equipment continually emerging. Engaging regularly in coaching sessions, attending clinics, and seeking feedback from experienced players are all critical for staying updated with the latest developments and learning new skills. These learning opportunities will help improve your technical abilities and broaden your understanding of the game, making your practice sessions more effective and your tournament experiences more rewarding.

Celebrating milestones and achievements—no matter how small—plays a critical role in sustaining your passion and motivation for pickleball. Whether it's reaching a new personal best in a skill drill, winning against a tough opponent, or simply playing your first tournament, taking time to acknowledge and celebrate these achievements can provide a significant emotional and motivational boost. Stop and give yourself a high five every time you succeed. Organize small personal celebrations or share these achievements with friends, family, or your pickleball community.

As this chapter concludes, reflect on how far you've come in your pickleball experience and the exciting possibilities that lie ahead. With clear goals, consistent practice, and a commitment to learning, you are well on your way to not just playing pickleball, but truly excelling at it. As you move forward, carry with you the lessons learned, the skills developed, and the joy that pickleball brings into each game.

TELL THEM TO "JUST DINK IT!"

The thought that you now have everything you need to shine on the court fills me with joy. Having seen how pickleball has changed countless lives for the better by boosting fitness and providing them with countless opportunities to expand their social circles, my aim is to let as many people about this easy yet engaging sport. Whether this book has inspired you to play for the first time, hone your serve or advanced shots, or even host a pickleball event of your own, I hope you can share your enthusiasm with others.

By letting them know how easy and vibrant pickleball is, you'll inspire them to commence an activity that could add years to their lives and help them build wonderful memories with family and friends, both old and new.

TAKE A MOMENT TO SHARE YOUR THOUGHTS!

I appreciate your help. Pickleball is paradise, and you can help others find it.

Scan the QR code below

CONCLUSION

Congratulations! You've reached the end of our comprehensive pickleball guide.

The foundation of your Pickleball prowess, as we've discovered, lies in a solid understanding of its basics. Remember, the history, rules, equipment, and fundamental techniques of Pickleball are the bedrock on which you will continue to build and refine your skills. I hope this book simplified and clarified the rules of the game for you.

Moreover, the role of physical and mental preparation cannot be overstressed. As you've learned, maintaining your physical fitness through targeted exercises, coupled with mental strategies to enhance focus and resilience, significantly elevates your game. Proper nutrition and injury prevention can ensure that every game you play contributes positively to your overall well-being.

CONCLUSION

Remember, this is an ongoing process. Practice, practice, practice. The drills, the use of modern technology, and the invaluable feedback from coaches or peers are tools that sharpen your techniques and strategic thinking. They are your allies in the quest to master the game and ascend to new levels of play. If you hit a plateau, don't be discouraged! I believe that you can push through and become an even better player.

Pickleball, as we've seen, is more than just a game—it's a vibrant community. Engaging with this community through clubs, tournaments, and social events can amplify your enjoyment and knit lasting bonds of friendship. It can bring your family together and provide a space for you to bond and keep active.

Take a moment to reflect on how far you've come. Celebrate your achievements, no matter how small they may seem, for each is a testament to your dedication and love for the game. Looking forward, set new objectives that excite you and push your boundaries even further.

So, grab your paddle and step onto the court with a heart full of enthusiasm and a mind eager to learn. Pickleball offers a unique blend of fitness, fun, and friendship—embrace these gifts.

Thank you for joining me on this journey. Your commitment to learning and improving in Pickleball is inspiring, and it is what will make you not just a player but a cherished member of the Pickleball community.

If you found this guide useful in understanding the rules of pickleball, improving your gameplay, or helping you find the confidence to join the community, then please leave a positive review. Doing so will help spread this information further and help more and more people reap the rewards of pickleball.

Keep swinging, keep playing, and most importantly, keep enjoying every moment of your Pickleball journey.

REFERENCES

11 Six 24 Pickleball. 2023. "Playing Pickleball in Different Weather Conditions: How to Adapt and Improve Your Game." June 4, 2023. https://11six24.com/blogs/pickleball/playing-pickleball-in-different-weather-conditions-how-to-adapt-and-improve-your-game.

Altru. 2023. "5 Common Pickleball Injuries & How to Prevent Them." *Altru Orthopaedics and Sports Medicine* (blog). August 8, 2023. https://www.altru.org/blog/2023/august/5-common-pickleball-injuries-how-to-prevent-them.

Asics. 2021. "6 Winning Ways Athletes Mentally Prepare for Competition." February 25, 2021. https://www.asics.com/us/en-us/blog/6-winning-ways-athletes-mentally-prepare-for-competition/.

Chertoff, Jane. 2019. "The Benefits of Dynamic Stretching and How to Get Started." Healthline. May 23, 2019. https://www.healthline.com/health/exercise-fitness/dynamic-stretching.

Cronkleton, Emily. 2019. "How and When to Include Static Stretching in Your Workout." Healthline. July 29, 2019. https://www.healthline.com/health/exercise-fitness/static-stretching.

Denahn, Shaun. n.d. "Mastering Pickleball Lobs: Strategies for Outsmarting Your Opponents." *The Skilled Pickle* (blog). https://www.theskilledpickle.com/blog/pickleball-lobs.

Edwards, Travis. 2022. "How to Build Muscle Strength: A Complete Guide." Healthline. April 1, 2022. https://www.healthline.com/health/fitness/how-to-build-strength-guide.

Fairgrounds. 2023. "Pickleball: The Game Going Viral on Social Media." December 16, 2023. https://www.visitfairgrounds.com/blog/pickleball-and-social-media.

Fergus, Tim. n.d. "Ultimate Tournament Recovery Methods – What Does the Science Say?" *The UAP* (blog). https://www.theuap.com/blog/ultimate-tournament-recovery-methods-what-does-the-science-say.

Flamm, Jason. 2024. "Improve Your Pickleball Footwork with This Technique." The Dink. May 9, 2024. https://www.thedinkpickleball.com/improve-your-pickleball-footwork-with-this-technique/.

Frazier, Kelly R. 2024. "How to Host a Pickleball Tournament with Friends,

Families, or Clubs." *Pickleball Central* (blog). January 2, 2024. https://pickleballcentral.com/blog/how-to-host-a-pickleball-tournament-with-friends-family-or-at-clubs/.

Gopal, Amy, and Shelly Shepard. 2024. "RICE Methods for Injuries." WebMD. April 24, 2024. https://www.webmd.com/first-aid/rice-method-injuries.

Grissom, Brynn. 2024. "Tips for playing pickleball with your family members." *Selkirk* (blog). February 9, 2024. https://www.selkirk.com/blogs/pickleball-education/tips-for-playing-pickleball-with-your-family-members.

IntoPickleball. n.d. "Kitchen Rules: What You Need to Know About the Non-Volley Zone." https://intopickleball.com/kitchen-rules-what-you-need-to-know-about-the-non-volley-zone/.

IZEA. 2023. "Pickleball Influencers Sharing the Game on Social Media." February 3, 2023. https://izea.com/resources/top-pickleball-influencers/.

Luxe Pickleball. 2024. "Mastering the Transition: Offensive and Defensive Strategies in Pickleball." *LUXE Pickleball* (blog). April 14, 2024. https://luxepickleball.com/blogs/news/mastering-the-transition-offensive-and-defensive-strategies-in-pickleball.

Noel, Brett. 2021. *Drills to Improve Your Pickleball Game Designed with 4 Players.* Coachable Pickleball. https://files.trackie.com/uploads/redactor/2021-02-28-21-45-09-1109555604-356.pdf.

Onix Pickleball. n.d. "The History of Pickleball." https://www.onixpickleball.com/blogs/learn-pickleball/the-history-of-pickleball.

Paddletek. n.d.-a. "9 Tips to Improve Pickleball Volleys." https://www.paddletek.com/blogs/news/better-pickleball-volleys.

———. n.d.-b. "How Do You Defend in Pickleball? 9 Tips." https://www.paddletek.com/blogs/news/9-defensive-pickleball-tips.

———. n.d.-c. "Pickleball Courts 101: The Ultimate Guide." https://www.paddletek.com/blogs/news/pickleball-courts-101.

———. n.d.-d. "Pickleball Etiquette: 19 Unspoken Rules for Newcomers." https://www.paddletek.com/blogs/news/pickleball-etiquette.

———. n.d.-e. "Pickleball Near Me: Finding Local Pickleball Courts." https://www.paddletek.com/blogs/news/pickleball-near-me.

———. n.d.-f. "Senior Pickleball Players - 7 Most Common Beginner Questions." https://www.paddletek.com/blogs/news/senior-pickleball-questions.

Paula, Donna. 2020. "5 Ways to Measure Your Improvement in Sports." Off

REFERENCES | 177

the Record Sports. September 29, 2020. https://offtherecordsports.com/5-ways-to-measure-your-improvement-in-sports/.

Pickleball University. 2022. "8 Strategies to Improve Your Pickleball Defense." March 28, 2022. https://www.pickleballuniversity.com/home/8-strategies-to-improve-your-pickleball-defense.

PrimeTime Pickleball. n.d.-a. "5 Best Pickleball Serves to Master (Beginner to Advanced)." https://primetimepickleball.com/best-pickleball-serves/.

———. n.d.-b. "This NEW Offensive Tactic Has Totally Revolutionized Pickleball Strategy." https://primetimepickleball.com/new-offensive-tactic-has-revolutionized-pickleball-strategy/.

———. n.d.-c. "What Is a Smash in Pickleball (Keys to Winning the Match)." https://primetimepickleball.com/what-is-a-smash-in-pickleball/.

PT & Me. 2023. "What to Eat Before, During, and after a Game." March 8, 2023. https://ptandme.com/blog/what-to-eat-before-during-after-a-game/.

Racket Royalty. 2023. "5 Ways to Practice Pickleball Alone." January 7, 2023. https://racketroyalty.com/blog/pickleball/how-to-practice-pickleball-alone/.

Read, Tyler. 2021. "The 8 Best Agility Exercises You Can Do at Home." Healthline. April 23, 2021. https://www.healthline.com/health/fitness/agility-exercises.

Rothermel, Andrew. 2019. "How to Design Sport Specific Training Programs." BioLane. January 27, 2019. https://biolayne.com/articles/training/how-to-design-sport-specific-training-programs/.

Shields, Thomas. 2023. "Feeling Targeted? Use the 'Squeeze' Pickleball Strategy." The Dink. January 18, 2023. https://www.thedinkpickleball.com/squeeze-pickleball-strategy/.

Shop the Courts. n.d. "Essential Two-Person Pickleball Drills for Skill Enhancement." https://www.shopthecourts.com/blogs/blog/essential-pickleball-drills-for-skill-enhancement.

Slowinski, Matt. 2023. "Mastering the Art of Perfect Serve Returns in Pickleball." *SportsEdTV* (blow). October 24, 2023. https://sportsedtv.com/blog/mastering-the-art-of-perfect-serve-returns-in-pickleball.

Strachan, Andre. 2019. "Andre Strachan's view on Targeted Play." Pickleball England. December 2, 2019. https://www.pickleballengland.org/andre-strachans-view-on-targeted-play/.

Straw, Eli. 2023. "Sports Psychology Focus Techniques." Success Starts Within. November 10, 2023. https://www.successstartswithin.com/

sports-psychology-articles/focus-training-for-sports/sports-psychology-focus-techniques/.

The Dink Media Team. 2023a. "5 Tips to Improve Your Pickleball Backhand | Guide to All Backhand Shots." The Dink. November 20, 2023. https://www.thedinkpickleball.com/pickleball-backhand-guide/.

———. 2023b. "New Study Reveals 36.5 Million People Played Pickleball Last Year." The Dink. January 5, 2023. https://www.thedinkpickleball.com/app-participation-report-2023/.

SlogansHub. "30 Pickleball Quotes." LinkedIn. March 29, 2024. https://www.linkedin.com/pulse/30-pickleball-quotes-sloganshub-q8dtf/

Townsend, Stacie. 2021. "11 Steps to Hitting the Perfect Pickleball Dink." The Pickler (blog). November 15, 2021. https://thepickler.com/pickleball-blog/perfect-pickleball-dink/.

Unsicker, Brayden. 2022. "A Pickleball Paddle Buyer's Guide: How to Pick the Right Paddle for You." Pickleball Effect (blog). June 21, 2022. https://pickleballeffect.com/other/a-pickleball-paddle-buyers-guide-how-to-pick-the-right-paddle-for-you/.

USAP. 2023. "Rules Summary." https://usapickleball.org/wp-content/uploads/2023/02/USA-Pickleball-Rules-Summary-_2_7_23.pdf.

———. 2024. "Suggested USA Pickleball Rule Changes for 2025." March 13, 2024. https://rules.usapickleball.org/entry/1433/.

———. n.d.-a. "History of the Game." https://usapickleball.org/what-is-pickleball/history-of-the-game/.

———. n.d.-b. "Strategies – Doubles Strategies." https://usapickleball.org/what-is-pickleball/strategies/doubles-strategies/.

VMKON Sport. n.d. "Pickleball Court Dimensions." https://vmkonsport.com/pickleball-court-dimensions/

West, Missy. 2016. "Overcoming a Plateau as an Athlete." Medium (blog). October 25, 2016. https://medium.com/@MissyWest25/overcoming-a-plateau-as-an-athlete-380ffd5d9d6b.

Yetman, Daniel. 2020. "What's the Difference Between Endurance and Stamina?" Healthline. June 12, 2020. https://www.healthline.com/health/exercise-fitness/endurance-vs-stamina.

Zhuo, Eric. 2023. "Pickleball for Kids: Tips and Tricks to Get Children Involved." Big Dill Pickleball Co. (blog). July 18, 2023. https://www.bigdillpickleballcompany.com/blogs/news/pickleball-for-kids-tips-and-tricks-to-get-children-involved.

Printed in Great Britain
by Amazon

7c08f44b-49a9-4791-9053-66255061a96aR01